God's Perfect Timing

A Literal Approach to Chronology in the Bible

Melvin J. Woodard III

SPEAK
IT TO
BOOK

Unless otherwise noted, all Scripture quotations are taken from the Holy Bible, New International Version®. Copyright © 1973, 1978, 1984, 2011 by Biblica, Inc.® Used by permission. All rights reserved worldwide.

Scripture quotations marked (NKJV) are taken from the New King James Version®. Copyright © 1982 by Thomas Nelson, Inc. Used by permission. All rights reserved.

Scripture quotations marked (NLT) are taken from the *Holy Bible*, New Living Translation, copyright © 1996, 2004, 2015 by Tyndale House Foundation. Used by permission of Tyndale House Publishers, Inc., Carol Stream, Illinois 60188. All rights reserved.

Speak It To Book
www.speakittobook.com

God's Perfect Timing / Melvin J. Woodard III
ISBN-13: 978-1-945793-92-9

This book is dedicated to those members of the body of Christ who call me "Pastor."

CONTENTS

Truth in the Word

I have done many things in my sixty years of life, including the practice of anesthesia for twenty-five years, pastoral ministry for over twenty-five years, and now—in my waning years of working in public life—teaching high school biology and science at Charles A. Tindley Accelerated (High) School in Indianapolis.

Right now, I am teaching a unit on ecology to my biology classes. We are studying population growth in ecosystems and using the population growth formula $P = P_0 \times e^{rT}$, where P = total population after time T, P_0 = starting population, r = % rate of growth, T = time in hours or years, and e = Euler number = 2.71828....

As I was teaching this unit, it dawned on me to try something: What would the world population be if the flood occurred in 2688 BC and eight people survived to repopulate the earth?

The flood occurred in 2688 BC, and Noah and his family of seven emerged from the ark to start a new world order in 2687 BC, one year later. Since then, the world population has grown from eight people to 7.7 billion people as of September 2019. Assuming a mere 0.484% growth rate on average throughout the 4,706 years since Noah and his family emerged from the flood, the Bible can be trusted to support the math and the current world population.

The equation looks like this:

$$P = P_0 \text{ x } e^{rT} \rightarrow 7,700,000,000 = 8 \text{ x } 2.71828^{0.00484 \text{ x } 4706}$$
$$P = 7,700,000,000$$
$$P_0 = 8$$
$$e = 2.71828$$
$$r = 0.00484 \ (0.484\%)$$
$$T = 4,706 \text{ years (time from 2687 BC to AD 2019).}$$

Check the math for yourself. If you're careful to put the right numbers in the correct places, you will find that the Bible is its own witness. Our current world population is exacted by the biblical witness of the flood.

I love the Lord, and I love to read His Word. God cannot lie and will not lie. His Word is filled with truth if we would mine it. Too often, we skim over truth and merely keep repeating phrases we have heard all our lives.

Thank you for continuing to read and discover more truth in God's Word along with me!

—*Dr. Mel Woodard*

INTRODUCTION

God's Timetable

We are creatures of time. It affects every moment of our lives. Yet when we study the Bible, our focus tends to be on principles and personalities rather than on how the events of redemptive history were perfectly timed by God. Since my own study of the Bible's timeline opened my eyes to some of God's big truths, my goal is to introduce as many people as possible to the rich experience of studying Scripture with a focus on God's timing.

Second Peter 3:8 states, "But, beloved, do not forget this one thing, that with the Lord one day is as a thousand years, and a thousand years as one day" (NKJV). Whether the time frame is accurate or not, this passage suggests that a day of time is much different for God from how it is for us, His creation. It is hard for me to comprehend how a day is like a thousand years and a thousand years are like a day, but that is how it appears to God.

The Almighty stands outside of time. He created time and operates within it when He chooses. God can move in and out of time as He desires. Wayne Grudem rightfully states, "It is evident throughout Scripture that God acts within time and acts differently at different points in time."[1]

Genesis 1:26 tells us that man was created in the image and likeness of God. Despite having been created in God's image, mankind was predestined to spend a finite amount of time on earth, as we learn from Genesis 6:3: "And the LORD said, 'My Spirit shall not strive with man forever, for he is indeed flesh; yet his days shall be one hundred and twenty years'" (NKJV). According to this scripture, God limits the lifespan of men to fewer than 120 years due to the presence of sin in the world. We spend a lot of this time waiting for God to act!

God Almighty uses time in different ways. Sometimes He uses it to discipline His children. As He did with the Israelites on many occasions, God will put us in "time-out" situations to discipline us, to slow us down, and to make adjustments in our lives.

God also uses time to display His mighty power. For instance, in troubled times we experience the grace and mercy of God, reminding us that trouble doesn't last forever. Times of difficulty can teach us about God's sovereignty. Whether for our good or God's ultimate glory, time is a tool in the hand of God.

Walking through life necessitates time and waiting on the Lord. Waiting for God to act is an inescapable part of life. It's even a spiritual imperative. Hosea 12:6 says to "maintain love and justice, and wait for your God always." What the Bible doesn't tell us is how long we'll be waiting. Time should be seen from God's perspective, not ours.

The Bible records what God has done in the past and what He plans to do in the future to bring us to salvation. If we study Scripture well, we will discover a number of important things about how God operates. From the very beginning of human history, there was a need for a Savior (see Genesis 3:15). Although Jesus came nearly 2,000 years ago, we are waiting for Him to return and finish what He started.

The church needs to be awake when Jesus Christ returns. We don't want to be like the disciples who fell asleep in the garden of Gethsemane, failing to pray and keep watch with Jesus (Matthew 26:36–46). If we're spiritually asleep when Jesus returns, we will miss one of the greatest moments in the history of the world.

This is why it's crucial for us to pay attention to the Bible's timeline. The purpose of this book is to give you important keys to help you better understand God's plan and His character through studying the time frame of Scripture. At the end of each chapter, a workbook section will give you the tools to explore how God's perfect timing throughout history is relevant to your life today.

God is marching methodically through His Word. The book of Revelation tells us that God's Word has not come to an end yet, but the end is approaching. We must use the precious time we have to reach the lost—those who have yet to receive Jesus Christ, the Son of God, Savior of the world.

I was a doctoral student when I first began to dive into the literal timing of the Bible. I was so fascinated by it that I often ignored my studies to focus on understanding God's timeline throughout His Word.

I've put years of study into this, and I firmly believe in it. You might not agree with my reasoning for dating things as I have, but keep in mind that the Bible isn't a history textbook in any conventional sense. There are details that aren't explained as fully and neatly as we would like.

The more I've studied, the more I've learned about how God works throughout time, which has taught me to be patient and endure difficult circumstances with a sense of hope and expectancy. Through my study of God's timing, I have become a different person—a person who knows and trusts that God will act when He is ready according to His timetable, not mine.

I hope this book will do the same for you. May God open your eyes to the wonders of His perfect timing as you read on.

CHAPTER ONE

Time Matters

Numbers are an important part of understanding the Bible. They enhance the story and provide a level of factual information and accuracy that words alone do not provide. Let's take the six days of creation as an example.

For in six days the LORD made the heavens and the earth, the sea, and all that is in them, but he rested on the seventh day. Therefore the LORD blessed the Sabbath day and made it holy.

—Exodus 20:11

I remember reading the first chapter of Genesis as a child and thinking, "God did all that work in six days? Really?" I didn't realize then that questions surrounding the creative activity of God would plague my spirit and start me on a lifelong theological journey. What is an accurate way to look at the creation story? Did God actually make the world in six, 24-hour days? If He did, how does science match up with the Bible's account?

Science suggests that the earth is much older than we are truly able to understand. Scientific discussions tend to create a division between people who are scientifically minded and those who are biblically minded. The scientifically minded think that the Bible's version of creation cannot be totally believed and accepted. Creationists, people who embrace the Bible's version of creation, claim that it is impossible to accept what science teaches about how the world was made.

I look at things in a different way. While we certainly have a great and powerful God who can bring about whatever He desires when He desires it, He may not have created the world in six, 24-hour days. He could have purposefully created the world gradually, adding man to the world at the end of His great, methodical creative process. This said, the age of the earth does not have to coexist with the presence of mankind. In other words, the length of human history does not have to equal the age of the earth.

It would be helpful to look at the book of Jude to understand my point. Jude consists of only one chapter and is divided into two neat parts, with verses 4–16 focusing on the dangers of false teachers and verses 17–25 focusing on the duty to defend God's truth. Verses 14–15 are pivotal because they shrink the dating process for the length of human history in a way that is very important to understand:

Enoch, the seventh from Adam, prophesied about them: "See, the Lord is coming with thousands upon thousands of his holy ones to judge everyone, and to convict all of them

*of all the ungodly acts they have committed in their ungod-
liness, and of all the defiant words ungodly sinners have
spoken against him.* "

—Jude 1:14–15

Why are these verses important? Because they offer us
numbers that we can work with to unlock the Scriptures.
Enoch is "the seventh from Adam" (Jude 1:14; Genesis
5:3–21). Based on the system of calculations I've drawn
from Scripture, Enoch lived from 3722–3357 BC. Jude,
the half-brother of Jesus Christ, wrote his epistle in AD
65, less than 3,500 years after Enoch lived. In historical
terms, this really is a small amount of time.

Given that a first-century follower of Jesus Christ,
Jude, was writing about an Old Testament patriarch,
Enoch, born in 3722 BC—about 3,400 years before him—
we know that the story must have been passed down
orally. Had Enoch lived 30,000 years before Jude, it's
highly likely that the story would have been lost. A gap of
3,000 years is historically meaningful.

From these verses in Jude, I naturally went back to
Genesis 5 and read through the history from Adam to
Noah. The lifespans of ten patriarchs are recounted by
Moses, the author of Genesis. Enoch is right there in the
seventh position (Genesis 5:21–24).

Looking at Jude 1:14–15 leads to an essential question:
Why did Jude feel it necessary to recall the work of Enoch
when he addressed the dangers of false teachers and the
importance of defending God's truth? Despite the passing
of 3,000+ years, life on earth has not changed much. False
teachers, liars, and doubters of God and His Word were in

existence then and still are now. Jude understood the need for those who love God to be ready to defend the Scriptures, as do those of us living now who call ourselves Christians. When we understand Scripture and dates, then we have an accurate picture of what God's Word is truly telling us, and we can put things in perspective.

A Heritage of Truth

My parents instilled two important values in me: a love for truth and a love for God's Word. When I was born—the second of five children and the first boy—my father had just graduated from Virginia Theological Seminary in Roanoke, Virginia, and was beginning a co-pastorate with his father in Chillicothe, Ohio. My parents expected that all of their children would tell the truth and live honest lives. They also expected their children to grow up and share the story of the Bible faithfully and accurately with others.

I spent many hours with my father, and occasionally with my grandfather, studying the Word of God. They always encouraged me to dig into the Bible and to discover as much truth as possible. "Read as best you can," I was told, "and the Holy Spirit will enlighten your understanding. As you get older, the Word will become nearer and dearer to you."

I was baptized at the age of 12 and accepted the call to ministry at the age of 22. I accepted my first pastorate at the age of 35, after I had engaged in a lengthy period of Bible study and seminary work. I had an unquenchable desire to know the deeper things of God and to understand

His Word as best as humanly possible. Knowing that I stood accountable to God, I wanted to understand His Word so I could teach my future congregations with wisdom and accuracy.

As I continue to live by the Spirit of God and reflect on various segments of the timeline in God's Holy Word, my spirit tells me that I have stumbled onto something great—something that will help me grow in faith and knowledge.

The Turning Point

It wasn't until I began working toward a doctorate in pulpit communication that I discovered the importance of chronology in Scripture. As with most doctoral programs, the first few years were consumed with classes, followed by years of research and study on a dissertation subject. I got lost in the chronology of Scripture during the research phase, and it became more important to me than my doctorate.

During those early days of my chronology research, I was introduced to an all-important date in Scripture, which gave rise to a particular timeline:

> *In the four hundred and eightieth year after the Israelites came out of Egypt, in the fourth year of Solomon's reign over Israel, in the month of Ziv, the second month, he began to build the temple of the LORD.*
>
> **—1 Kings 6:1**

The professor used 966 BC as the date for this verse. Using the date of 966 BC and reflecting upon other scriptures—passages like Genesis 5, with its genealogy from Adam to Noah, and Genesis 11, with its genealogy from Shem to Abram—helped me to put the story of the Bible together like I had never done before. I gained a deeper understanding of how God works within creation.

I originally took my professor's knowledge of the 966 BC date at face value and considered it to be truth. As I began researching the chronology of the Bible for myself, my research would lead me to agree wholeheartedly with the date of 966 BC for 1 Kings 6:1. I also realized that I could work my way back to a date for Adam in the Garden of Eden. It may sound far-fetched, but it really is possible.

A brief word is needed here in determining the date of 1 Kings 6:1 as 966 BC. It is based on knowing several other pieces of information. First, an eclipse occurred on June 15, 763 BC that has been used to help fix dates for most of the Assyrian kings.[2] Second, the Battle of Qarqar, in which the Assyrians fought against the Arameans, occurred in the sixth year of Shalmaneser III's reign, in 853 BC.[3] Third, Solomon began to build his temple in the fourth year of his reign, and the temple was constructed from 966–959 BC. Solomon's reign lasted from 970–931 BC.[4]

In my spiritual journey of growth, I no longer ignore dates and time in the Word of God. It has now become habitual for me to trace time in the Word, because dating texts brings a fuller understanding to Scripture. When I'm working on a sermon and a date appears, I ask myself, "How does this impact what I already know?"

As I mentioned, my chronology research became more important to me than my doctorate, so I didn't finish my dissertation. I found more value in my research of dating the Bible, as it provided me with a better understanding of God's Word. Of all the educational experiences I've undertaken in my life, and there have been many, the doctorate in pulpit communication was the only one I didn't fully complete. That's how important the timeline of God's Word became to me.

In a way, this book is the dissertation I was not able to finish. Instead of dealing with pulpit communication, it focuses on my true passion: the chronology of Scripture. All of this work drives me toward one lofty question: Where are we on God's divine timeline now, in 2019? A whole lot of other questions come to me as soon as I ask this one. It just may be that the end of the church age is nearer than we think.

Numbers in Operation

Numbers and time have been important to me for a very long while. In my previous career as an anesthesiologist assistant, working inside operating rooms across northeast Ohio for about twenty-five years, time and numbers were continually woven into my daily routine. While working within surgical teams in those operating rooms on behalf of thousands of patients, I couldn't help but think about how much time God has gifted to each member of creation.

During my career, I administered cardiothoracic anesthesia extensively, working with infants and toddlers all the way up to patients in their eighties and nineties. I would piece together their stories as I sought answers to questions like, "How did they end up on an operating table? Why did this happen to them?" Medically speaking, we could find plenty of reasons. But in God's eternal plan, why did it happen?

I realized that God is sovereign and allows things to happen in each person's life at whatever age is determined. The sovereignty of God is a mystery to us. This kind of thinking typically has led me to ponder my own mortality and wonder what God has in store for my life. All has not yet been made known.

Numbers mean something in the world of anesthesia. How much anesthesia you administer to a patient depends on the person's height, weight, age, and other quantifiable factors. The patient's heart rate and blood pressure need to be monitored and recorded in the patient's medical notes. Medication dosages need to be tailored to each individual patient to help alleviate symptoms as much as possible while also reducing the possibility of side effects. It was crucial for me to be accurate with numbers, times, and dates and how they impacted a patient's medical condition.

Because of my work as an anesthesiologist assistant, I developed a habit of thinking about characters in the Bible the same way. I became curious about where biblical personalities were in their lives (age, date, time, and so forth) when events happened, and I also wanted to know what God said to those He addressed. This kind of activity alleviates some guesswork because we do not study deeper than what is presented.

Take Jesus for example. The Bible says, "Now Jesus himself was about thirty years old when he began his ministry" (Luke 3:23). Why does the Bible include such a specific detail about Jesus' life? (More on this point later.) If the Bible makes pertinent details known to us, they absolutely mean something. As readers, we must follow up on these details.

In Luke 4:16–22, Jesus entered the synagogue on the Sabbath, read a passage from the prophet Isaiah, and then pronounced the scripture as being fulfilled in their presence. We know that the time of this passage was near the Day of Atonement in AD 26, and we know that Jesus had already celebrated his thirtieth birthday. Based on information recorded in the Gospels, Jesus' ministry lasted about three and a half years, until the Passover in AD 30. This information helps us understand that Jesus died at the age of 33.

There is nothing coincidental with God. For the Israelites to enter the promised land, God's servants, Moses and Joshua, had to defeat thirty-three kings who inhabited the promised land—east and west of the Jordan River. God promised Abraham that He would give this land to the children of God, the Jews, and He certainly provided it with the help of His servants.

I don't think it is coincidental that Jesus Christ lived and died, conquering the enemy of God's people, in thirty-three years. As the ultimate Servant of God, Jesus led the defeat of the enemy so the children of God, both Jews and gentiles, could inhabit the promised land. In God's perfect time, He honored His word and provided eternal blessings for His children.

The Bible offers us limited information about the first thirty years of Jesus' life. Why? Because what is most important is Jesus' ministry on behalf of His Father, which culminated in His death on the cross to secure the salvation of men. We are continually challenged to keep our eyes on God the Father, having watched Him work out His divine purpose and plan in the life of Jesus Christ. The same is true of our lives. We need to keep our eyes on God and watch Him work His purpose and plan through us.

We all will experience pivotal moments when God leads us into a new season of ministry or gives us a new assignment. For me, that happened when God called me out of the medical field and into pastoring. In making that transition, I brought with me a love of numbers, dates, and times.

A Taste of God's Timing in Scripture

While God's truths are timeless, the events of the Bible happened in real time. Every time I read a passage of Scripture, I consider its date and how that information enhances what I already understand of Scripture.

Going back to our earlier example in the book of Jude, it is interesting to note that Jude was not a follower of Jesus while He walked the earth (John 7:5). Jude became a follower only after Jesus' death and resurrection (Acts 1:14). Did the resurrection of Jesus make that much of a difference in Jude's life that he decided to follow Christ?

Obviously, we cannot underestimate the impact of the resurrection and how significant this fact was in building the early church. Without the resurrection, there is no faith, no church of Jesus Christ, and no eternal salvation. However, I muse over the fact that Jude is writing—thirty-five years after Jesus' death—about false teachers trying to tear down what Jesus put together. Enemies of the cross appeared very quickly, according to the biblical narrative, and they still exist today. However, Jude, once an enemy of the cross, had become a follower and leading voice of Christ. The death of his half-brother changed his whole life in less than thirty-five years. That right there demonstrates the power of the cross.

The Acts of the Apostles is another example of the need to understand time and dates. Dates help us better understand the life and work of the New Testament's great apostle Paul. Acts provides detailed information on Paul's missionary journeys, allowing us to understand the timing of his travels. From a dating standpoint, it would be helpful to know when Paul was converted and became a follower of Jesus Christ (AD 33). Since we can date Paul and his various journeys, we should be able to determine a date for his conversion.

By looking at dates, we can see a clear picture of Paul's transformational journey and his perseverance in the mission, from approving of the stoning of Stephen (AD 32, Acts 7:57–8:1) and persecuting the early church (AD 33, Acts 8:3) to proclaiming the gospel to the gentiles during three missionary journeys (AD 47–58, Acts 13:1–21:16) and, finally, being willing to die for spreading the news of Jesus in Rome (AD 67/68, Acts 21:17–28:31). The life of the apostle Paul is a whirlwind of activity and covers more than thirty years.

Within three decades, Paul became the go-to apostle for theological matters, and we have to ask ourselves how and why. Time created this walk of faith and power in his life, and the same is true for us as we read the Bible with increasing understanding and a timeline in our minds and hearts.

The authors of the various books in the Bible were people experiencing real life in the moment. Their experiences shaped their understanding and perspectives on the things they decided to share with us, which is why timing is so relevant to understanding their stories. We gain more insight into the Bible when we know when portions of Scripture were written and when the events being written about took place.

Of course, one can read the Bible without any knowledge of time and dates, and it can still make sense. However, when Isaiah wrote, "Therefore the Lord himself will give you a sign: The virgin will conceive and give birth to a son, and will call him Immanuel" (Isaiah 7:14), it helps to know that Isaiah was not speaking about Jesus a few days before He was born. Isaiah was, in fact, prophesying Jesus' birth almost 700 years before it actually happened. Accurate prophecy gives credence to the Word of God. We can believe every word we read.

What an incredible testimony to the sovereignty and omniscience of our God! Never do we need to doubt Him. My grandmother used to say, "He may not come when you want Him, but He will be there right on time." God's timing is perfect.

Get Ready

Dates are important. Time is important. If God, who is timeless, stepped into time for just over thirty-three years and said that He is coming back to reign on earth for 1,000 years (Revelation 20:4), we had better have an understanding of time.

Without an eye on time, we may find ourselves unprepared for Christ's return, like the five virgins who were waiting for the bridegroom but didn't have their lamps trimmed and burning (Matthew 25:1–13). The bridegroom's arrival caught the virgins by surprise, and they weren't ready to go with him. As a result, the door of opportunity was closed, and they were not able to go with the bridegroom into the wedding banquet. Having an understanding of the timeline of Scripture helps us to keep our lamps trimmed and burning as we wait expectantly for our Lord and Savior to return. He will one day establish His kingdom on earth for 1,000 years.

The dates and times that we shall bring forth from the Word of God are not tens of thousands of years ago. Adam and Eve lived a little more than 6,000 years ago, Abraham lived approximately 4,000 years ago, and Jesus Christ lived almost 2,000 years ago. Bible personalities lived close enough to us in history that we can believe their message and fully understand. I encourage you to use dates to help you dig deeper into the Bible, contend for your faith, and pass it on to our immediate generations so they can be ready when Jesus Christ returns.

Chapter One Questions

Question: What questions about the timing of biblical events have you always been curious about but never found the answers to? Commit to using this book as a springboard to deeper study of the Word, especially the topic of God's timing.

_____

_____

_____

_____

_____

_____

_____

_____

_____

_____

_____

Question: Describe some areas in your life where you have struggled with accepting God's perfect timing. What are some instances of waiting on God that you have been through in the past or are experiencing currently? How does understanding God as timeless, yet operating within time, help to shape your perspective on your own waiting seasons?

_____

_____

_____

_____

_____

_____

_____

_____

_____

_____

_____

_____

Action: Create a spiritual timeline of your own life. If your parents and/or grandparents were believers, include their conversions and other spiritual milestones in your heritage (e.g. the salvation of a spiritual mentor or the birth of the person who led you to Christ). Include the date of your own profession of faith, your baptism, and important events that have shaped your walk with the Lord, as well as major life events, such as marriage or the birth of a child. Thank God for how He has been at work throughout your life and even before you were born.

Chapter One Notes

_____

_____

_____

_____

_____

_____

_____

_____

_____

_____

_____

_____

_____

_____

_____

_____

_____

_____

_____

CHAPTER TWO

Man's Early Years

So, how do we start figuring out the timeline of Scripture? There are two scriptures that are important for us to embrace and fully understand: 1 Kings 6:1 and 2 Peter 3:8. Understand that the date of the former text is 966 BC, as mentioned in Chapter 1. We will return to this date in a moment. Let me address the latter text first. If 2 Peter 3:8 is taken literally, and I suggest that you try it before you deny it, this text can provide a key to how time works from God's perspective. Second Peter 3:8 states, "But, beloved, do not forget this one thing, that with the Lord one day is as a thousand years, and a thousand years as one day" (NKJV).

Although God exists outside of time, He is always present and very much involved in it. Occasionally, He will temporarily step into time to minister to His children, as He did in the Old Testament as the angel of the Lord or in the New Testament in the person of Jesus Christ. In addition to His divine attributes, omnipresent and eternal, God is also omnitemporal, meaning that He can move in and out of time as He desires.[5]

As a creature of time, it gives me a great sense of peace and comfort to know that the God I serve, the One who created me, respects time. If eternity were the only thing that mattered to Him, then my years on earth would have no value. I wholeheartedly believe that God understands the finite timeline of our lives.

Looking at 2 Peter 3:8 from a mathematic standpoint, if you take 1,000 and divide it by 24—the number of hours in a day—it comes out to 42 years (41.7 rounded up). To be clear, this means that 42 years equates to one hour with God. Hypothetically, we could deduce that every hour on God's clock equals about 42 years of our lives. If you take Peter's words literally, they yield a very interesting thought: God's time is not like our time. Years with us are but minutes with God. That's important to understand. Waiting on God takes time, a lot of it. He is not slow, as some people may think, but His timetable is not like ours.

Now, consider Genesis 6:3: "Then the LORD said, 'My Spirit will not contend with humans forever, for they are mortal; their days will be a hundred and twenty years.'" I love and embrace this radical thought; it reminds me that God will not tolerate human beings, who were all born as sinners, forever. God gives us plenty of time in our lives to say yes to salvation so that each of us might become a new creation. When we do say yes to God, then we want to seek Him out and spend time with Him.

However, God is holy and knows that the hearts of men are filled with desires that cause us to use our time in careless, frivolous, and silly ways. Too many of us waste time by walking in ways that aren't pleasing to God. He, therefore, doesn't give mankind a lot of time to waste. The vast majority of people don't make it to the 120-year limit. If I want the favor of the Lord and the ability to spend time in His presence, I have to become righteous like He is.

There are times and seasons in life when we cause ourselves grief and God decides that we need a time out—you know, like our parents did to us for five or ten minutes when we misbehaved. Well, according to God's clock, five minutes equals three and a half years, while ten minutes happens to be seven years. When you and I are going through dark and difficult days, fussing over situations and complaining about how long it's taking to come out on the other side, we can rest a little easier knowing how God works. A five- or ten-minute time out from God will consume three to seven years of our lives. This painful correction from the Lord can yield big dividends in our lives. He may need to change our ways, change our thoughts, or move us in a new direction. It takes time.

Waiting According to God's Clock

It's important that we respect time and make the effort to understand it a bit more from God's perspective. For one thing, it helps us to wait for Him more patiently. King David said it very well: "Wait on the LORD; be of good courage, and He shall strengthen your heart; wait, I say, on the LORD!" (Psalm 27:14 NKJV).

Waiting is an inevitable part of life and the Christian experience. Being creatures of time, we'd like to know how long we have to wait before God will move or resolve a difficult situation. But because time is different with God, we should find that we have greater endurance and perseverance in seasons of waiting. If God whispers for us to wait five minutes, it could very well be three or more years before we see the answer to our prayers.

I may tell God that I'm willing to wait ten minutes for Him, but am I truly prepared to wait? Ten minutes for Him is seven years for us. When we're looking at minutes, the Lord is looking at years.

> "For my thoughts are not your thoughts, neither are your ways my ways," declares the LORD. "As the heavens are higher than the earth, so are my ways higher than your ways and my thoughts than your thoughts."
> —Isaiah 55:8–9

As His thoughts and ways are not our thoughts and ways, God's timing is not our timing. Scientific evidence may indicate that the earth is billions of years old and that man has been around a very long time (tens of thousands of years), but it is my contention that the lineage of man is not as long as we are led to think. Based on my study of Scripture, the time frame from Adam to the present day has been a little more than 6,000 years.

I embrace the fact that our God, the Maker of the heavens and the earth, doesn't act solely within a 24-hour clock; His frame of time has a more eternal sense to it. There is benefit to this kind of understanding. This point enables you and me to endure years of life's difficulty—of growth, of raising children, of illness—with greater patience, love, and mercy. As a result, we become different creatures, creatures who are more like Christ.

An Eye-Opening Genealogy

When you read the Bible with God's perspective of time in mind, you'll find that you stop skipping over the genealogies. Instead of skimming them and wondering why God included them in His Word, you realize that they are the pillars and posts to our biblical foundation.

Let's consider the genealogy from Adam to Noah in Genesis 5. The first few verses establish a pattern that continues for the rest of the genealogy:

> *This is the written account of Adam's family line.*
>
> *When God created mankind, he made them in the likeness of God. He created them male and female and blessed them. And he named them "Mankind" when they were created.*
>
> *When Adam had lived 130 years, he had a son in his own likeness, in his own image; and he named him Seth. After Seth was born, Adam lived 800 years and had other sons and daughters. Altogether, Adam lived a total of 930 years, and then he died.*
>
> **—Genesis 5:1–5**

It's rather easy to get bogged down in all of the numbers and miss what this genealogy is trying to tell us. But when we assign dates to the lifetimes of these individuals, the passage comes alive. Here are the dates of the patriarchs, as I have calculated them based upon the date of 966 BC for 1 Kings 6:1:

- Adam (Genesis 5:3–5): 4344 BC–3414 BC

- Seth (Genesis 5:6–8): 4214 BC–3302 BC

- Enosh (Genesis 5:9–11): 4109 BC–3204 BC

- Kenan (Genesis 5:12–14): 4019 BC–3109 BC

- Mahalalel (Genesis 5:15–17): 3949 BC–3054 BC

- Jared (Genesis 5:18–20): 3884 BC–2922 BC

- Enoch (Genesis 5:21–24): 3722 BC–3357 BC

- Methuselah (Genesis 5:25–27): 3657 BC–2688 BC

- Lamech (Genesis 5:28–31): 3470 BC–2693 BC

- Noah (Genesis 5:32): 3288 BC–2338 BC.

As a note, Noah was 600 years old when the rainwater fell and the deep waters rose that covered the entire world (Genesis 7:6), which would date the flood at 2688 BC.

When I looked at this list of dates for the first time, I came to realize that many of these patriarchs' lives overlapped—they were alive during the same times. In fact, out of the ten patriarchs mentioned above, the only person who did not know Adam personally was Noah, who was born after Adam died. Talk about Scripture coming to life!

It's hard for us to wrap our heads around the fact that the first people lived for such long periods of time. The question of sin must be factored into all of this. Obviously, this was before God instituted the lifespan limit of 120 years in Genesis 6:3. There are a lot of questions to ponder for another time, but it's no coincidence that God allowed the first inhabitants to live as long as they did. There was a purpose.

God never leaves Himself without a witness. His story, with all of its divine glory and creative genius, needed to be passed down from one generation to another. Because the first people lived such long, generationally overlapping lives, they were able to pass down the story of our creation—the Garden of Eden, the fall of mankind, and the entrance of sin into our previously perfect world, changing humankind from innocent creatures to broken and distorted reflections of God's image. God's design for human beings allowed our story to be told from one generation to the next without being broken.

Looking at the date of Noah's birth (3288 BC), we realize that six of his forefathers—Enosh, Kenan, Mahalalel, Jared, Methuselah, and Lamech—were still alive at the time. Methuselah, Noah's grandfather, even lived right up to the time of the flood in 2688 BC. Noah probably would have heard Adam's story from various family members.

Only Noah, his wife, and his three sons and their wives survived the flood (Genesis 7:1). We can be confident that Noah knew what life had been like before the fall because his ancestors had told him. It is vital for us to recognize that we have an oral tradition of the world's beginning times, in addition to biblical manuscripts, to help increase our faith. Knowing that we still have a perfect record of our beginning, because the story was told enough that Noah could retell it, helps solidify my faith.

The genealogy in Genesis 5 shows us that God will

keep His story alive. He will utilize generations and orchestrate their lives and times so that His story is passed on in unbroken fashion. Future generations can be assured of the truth of God and His Word.

Knowledge of Scripture dates and timelines helps us to realize how close these people were to us in history. It makes the Bible smaller and easier to handle, and it shows us how important it is to understand everything from Genesis to Revelation.

The Need for a Savior

This raises the question, however, that if Adam's story was being passed down and shared, how did mankind become so wicked and corrupt (Genesis 6:5)? How was man's downward spiral into the grasp of sin possible when generations of people, living at the same time, had heard stories about the wonderful days of innocence of Adam and Eve in the Garden of Eden?

Just like us, the first people on earth had free will. Freedom of choice is the earmark of being human. Although we have been made in the image and likeness of God (Genesis 1:26), we are not forced to have a relationship with Him. The Lord allows us to decide for ourselves and choose whether or not to obey Him. We can make our own choices, go our own directions, and decide whether to be righteous like God or unrighteous like people without God. Our time on earth can profit the Kingdom of God, or it can be wasted on selfish concerns and desires. We need to recognize that the time God has given each of us is a gift.

We clearly see the need for a Savior as we read through the Word of God. Man is inevitably lost in sin when he is left to himself and his own devices (Romans 3:23). The Lord God sent His Son and our Savior, Jesus Christ, at the right time. With no other options left, Jesus had to come (Romans 5:6). Galatians 4:4–5 states, "But when the fullness of the time had come, God sent forth His Son, born of a woman, born under the law, to redeem those who were under the law, that we might receive the adoption as sons" (NKJV).

Even after the flood wiped the earth clean of all life forms, except those in the ark with Noah, it didn't take long for sin to rear its ugly head. Not long after the flood, Noah got drunk and laid naked in his tent. Ham saw the nakedness of his father, told his brothers, Shem and Japheth, and was cursed for his actions (Genesis 9:20–25).

At our very best, we make small, temporary advances in God's direction. Mankind needs a Savior. It was absolutely necessary for God to bridge that gap between Himself and man by sending His Son, Jesus Christ.

The Purpose of Mankind

From the first chapter of Genesis, we learn God's original purpose for mankind:

> God blessed them and said to them, "Be fruitful and increase in number; fill the earth and subdue it. Rule over the fish in the sea and the birds in the sky and over every living creature that moves on the ground."
> **—Genesis 1:28**

After God created the first human beings, He gave them this responsibility. Through those ten generations in Genesis 5, a portion of God's mandate was fulfilled. People multiplied and began to fill the earth. However, when mankind began to subdue the earth and exercise dominion over it, it was not for the glory of God and the renown of His name. They did it for their own good and glory.

As Genesis 6:5 states, "…every inclination of the thoughts of the human heart was only evil all the time." This grieved God's heart, and He regretted that He had created mankind (Genesis 6:6). Why? Because they didn't do what He had asked. He did not receive any glory from their works. They did everything for their own name and fame and to fulfill their own desires.

Paul emphasized the importance of working for the glory of God:

> *Whatever you do, work at it with all your heart, as working for the Lord, not for human masters, since you know that you will receive an inheritance from the Lord as a reward. It is the Lord Christ you are serving.*
> **—Colossians 3:23–24**

The apostle Paul's words reflect back to the beginning, when mankind was stealing God's glory and working for personal ends. If there's anything that draws the ire of God, it's when mankind is knowingly disobedient and resistant to giving Him glory, for God is the Author and Creator of life (Genesis 1:1; Psalm 24:1).

Mankind has had the opportunity to work for the glory of God ever since being expelled from the Garden of

Eden. Genesis 4:2 states that Cain, the ill-fated son of Adam and the brother of Abel, "worked the soil." It's clear that Abel had a choice: to please God or to please himself. Abel chose the latter and was reprimanded by God. God gives each of us the gift of life and time to do His bidding. We either give God His glory or we steal it from Him in self-pleasing ways. Our time on earth, here and now, is important.

In Genesis 4:17, we find that Cain built a city. Verse 22 tells us about Tubal-Cain, one of Cain's descendants, "who forged all kinds of tools out of bronze and iron." Mankind was building and creating. They were subduing the earth, but they were doing it for their own glory, not for the glory of God.

Consider this boast from Lamech, one of Cain's descendants:

> Lamech said to his wives, "Adah and Zillah, listen to me; wives of Lamech, hear my words. I have killed a man for wounding me, a young man for injuring me. If Cain is avenged seven times, then Lamech seventy-seven times."
> —*Genesis 4:23–24*

By his own words, Lamech was hardly focused on the glory of God. It appears easy for man to become arrogant and full of pride and lust because of what he is able to achieve. Life lived apart from God is less than the glorious plan God originally had in mind. Jesus Christ emphasized this truth when He said, "If you abide in Me, and My words abide in you, you will ask what you desire, and it shall be done for you. By this My Father is glorified, that you bear much fruit; so you will be My disciples" (John 15:7–8 NKJV).

Time Is Running Out

Let's return briefly to the story of creation in Genesis. The text clearly says that God created the heavens and the earth in six days. Believers readily accept this fact. However, rather than thinking of this as six, 24-hour days, consider the timeline in 2 Peter 3:8: "a day is like a thousand years, and a thousand years are like a day." I believe that God does not have to rush to do anything, because He stands outside of time and will use it to satisfy His will. (By the way, the real miracle of creation was not in the amount of time it took.) Looking at creation from the perspective that a day is 1,000 years, we learn that God took His time creating the earth and preparing man to tend to it.

Elsewhere, the Bible shows us that the timeline from Adam to Abraham was about 2,000 years, or two days; from Abraham to Jesus Christ was about 2,000 years, or two days; and from Jesus Christ to the present was about 2,000 years, or two days. Therefore, God moved from Adam to Christ to the present in a little more than 6,000 years, or six days, of time, which is the same as the original days of creation.

The Bible lets us know that the seventh day will begin when Christ returns and sits on His earthly throne, as prophesied in the book of Revelation. Being able to assign a date to Adam helps us to see the end of history clearly and prepare for Christ's return.

God will not contend with evil, sinful man forever (Genesis 6:3). After six days/6,000 years of God wrestling with mankind, the question remains as to who will choose to walk with Him and who will not. Those who choose to walk with Him will enjoy eternity with Him. Those who choose the other path will experience eternal damnation.

The time frame is tighter than we think; we don't have a lot of time to work with. The earth itself may be millions of years old as some scientists claim, but the biblical time frame of man covers only a little more than 6,000 years. Be careful not to get sidetracked by geological eras. Our focus needs to be on the chronology of Scripture.

Be Like Enoch

God is concerned about every human life He has brought into existence. He is looking to see who will choose to walk with Him and who will not. When we look at the genealogy in Genesis 5, it's evident that Enoch was the favored character in that particular part of the story:

> *When Enoch had lived 65 years, he became the father of Methuselah. After he became the father of Methuselah, Enoch walked faithfully with God 300 years and had other sons and daughters. Altogether, Enoch lived a total of 365 years. Enoch walked faithfully with God; then he was no more, because God took him away.*
> **—Genesis 5:21–24**

When God took Enoch away, I believe that was a sure sign to the rest of us. If we choose to walk with God, living a life that glorifies and pleases Him, He will take us to be with Him. If we choose not to walk with God, we will go the way of the unrighteous—we will die. Like Noah, get in the ark with God.

Jesus cautioned us, "Enter through the narrow gate. For wide is the gate and broad is the road that leads to destruction, and many enter through it. But small is the gate and narrow the road that leads to life, and only a few find it" (Matthew 7:13–14). If we choose to walk with God—if we accept Jesus Christ as our Lord and Savior and we love and obey Him—He will take us to be with Him one day, just like He did Enoch.

Of the ten patriarchs listed in Genesis 5, we are told that two of them found life: Enoch and Noah. They were righteous in God's eyes. It's difficult to know if the other eight chose to walk with God, but Scripture is clear that Enoch is someone to emulate. We should strive to be like him and walk with God through eternity.

Use Your Time Wisely

God gives each one of us a finite amount of time on this earth. It's extremely important that we use the time we are given wisely. If we waste our time and squander our lives, we may find ourselves missing out on a blissful eternity with the Lord.

Jesus said, "For whoever desires to save his life will lose it, but whoever loses his life for My sake will find it" (Matthew 16:25 NKJV). We must relinquish authority over our lives and turn them over to Christ. We need to let Him have our lives, our time. Our lives will not be as long as those of the antediluvian patriarchs, but whatever time we do have should be laid at the feet of our Lord and Savior.

WORKBOOK

Chapter Two Questions

Question: Do you believe that God respects time and cares about the finite time frame of your life? What evidence of this do you see in Scripture and in history? Contrast how a small child views time with how an older adult does. How does this provide insight into the vast difference between our view of time and God's?

_____

_____

_____

_____

_____

_____

_____

_____

_____

_____

_____

Question: What are some ways in which you are using your time on earth wisely (e.g. to help others come to Christ and to glorify God)? What are some empty or useless things on which you are wasting time? Do you manage your time with focus and direction, or do you let it manage you with frivolity and distraction?

_____

_____

_____

_____

_____

_____

_____

_____

_____

_____

_____

_____

Action: What does it mean to live and work for God's glory? Write out your personal definition. Commit Colossians 3:23–24 to memory. Dedicate yourself to using whatever time you have remaining in your life to work for

His glory and not your own desires.

Chapter Two Notes

CHAPTER THREE

Noah to Abraham

In the first 1,700 years of human history, it is clear that mankind did not use their time wisely. Genesis 5, from Adam (4344 BC) to Noah and his experience in the flood (2688 BC), records the timeline of ten early patriarchs. They had become so evil that God wanted to wipe them all out and start fresh.

> *The LORD saw how great the wickedness of the human race had become on the earth, and that every inclination of the thoughts of the human heart was only evil all the time. The LORD regretted that he had made human beings on the earth, and his heart was deeply troubled. So the LORD said, "I will wipe from the face of the earth the human race I have created—and with them the animals, the birds and the creatures that move along the ground—for I regret that I have made them."*
>
> **—Genesis 6:5–7**

It did not take mankind long to mess things up, especially when you consider time from God's perspective. To help you understand things from the alternate perspective, I will repeatedly refer to God's way of looking at time. For instance, 1,700 years amounts to roughly a day and a half of time. It only took about a day and a half for the human race to move from a pre-fall state of innocence to complete corruption.

No matter how bad things get with mankind, God always has a righteous remnant. During the early period, there was still one line of righteous men, for "Noah found favor in the eyes of the LORD" (Genesis 6:8). His line was preserved through the flood and provided the fresh start that mankind so badly needed. This is set out in detail for us in Genesis 11.

Mankind After the Flood

To work through the genealogy in Genesis 11, there are some dates you need to establish first:

- Abraham: 2166 BC–1991 BC (Genesis 11:26; 25:7)

- Isaac: 2066 BC–1886 BC (Genesis 12:5; 35:28)

- Jacob: 2006 BC–1859 BC (Genesis 25:26; 47:28)

- Joseph: 1915 BC–1805 BC (Genesis 41:46; 45:11; 47:28; 50:26)

- The Sojourn: 1876 BC–1446 BC (Exodus 12:40)

- The Exodus: 1446 BC–1406 BC (Deuteronomy 1:3).

(Please refer to Chapter 4 and Appendix A to learn more about how these dates were calculated.) It's easiest to work backward from the end of the chapter. If we know the dates of Abraham's life, we can date the life of his father, Terah. Genesis 11:32 tells us, "Terah lived 205 years, and he died in Harran." Using the life of Abraham, we know that Terah was born in 2236 BC. We can now work backward further through the rest of Shem's line. Genesis 11:26 says, "After Terah had lived 70 years, he became the father of Abram, Nahor and Haran." This would give Abraham a birth year of 2166 BC—seventy years after that of his father, Terah.

We can continue to fill in the birth years for the people in this genealogy by following the above pattern:

- Terah (Genesis 11:26–32): 2236 BC

- Nahor (Genesis 11:24–25): 2265 BC

- Serug (Genesis 11:22–23): 2295 BC

- Reu (Genesis 11:20–21): 2327 BC

- Peleg (Genesis 11:18–19): 2357 BC

- Eber (Genesis 11:16–17): 2391 BC

- Shelah (Genesis 11:14–15): 2421 BC

- Arphaxad (Genesis 11:12–13): 2456 BC

- Shem (Genesis 11:10–11): 2556 BC.

Now, if we look at the genealogy listed in Luke 3, we notice that there is a seeming discrepancy between Genesis 11 and Luke 3:

...the son of Serug, the son of Reu, the son of Peleg, the son of Eber, the son of Shelah, the son of Cainan, the son of Arphaxad, the son of Shem, the son of Noah, the son of Lamech....

—Luke 3:35–36

Cainan wasn't listed in the Genesis 11 genealogy, so where did he come from? It turns out that he was actually the father of Shelah and the son of Arphaxad. As a result, I need to adjust my dates for the genealogy in Genesis 11 and include Cainan:

- Terah (Genesis 11:26–32): 2236 BC

- Nahor (Genesis 11:24–25): 2265 BC

- Serug (Genesis 11:22–23): 2295 BC

- Reu (Genesis 11:20–21): 2327 BC

- Peleg (Genesis 11:18–19): 2357 BC

- Eber (Genesis 11:16–17): 2391 BC

- Shelah (Genesis 11:14–15): 2421 BC

- Cainan (Luke 3:36): 2551 BC

- Arphaxad (Genesis 11:12–13): 2686 BC

- Shem (Genesis 11:10–11): 2786 BC.

When we add Cainan into Shem's line, the birth years of some of these individuals change. Shelah's birth year of 2421 BC is still correct, but Cainan, who was his father, was born in 2551 BC. He was 130 years old when Shelah was born. This information is found in the Septuagint version of the Gospel of Luke, which I'll get into more later.

With the introduction of Cainan, I have to adjust the date for Arphaxad, who was the father of Cainan. The Septuagint tells us that he was 135 years old when Cainan was born, which puts Arphaxad's birth year at 2686 BC. That moves Shem's birth year to 2786 BC, because he was 98 years old when the flood occurred and 100 years old when Arphaxad was born.

Cainan's place in the genealogy is important because it gives us a more precise and accurate year for the flood: 2688 BC. If we purely use the dates in Genesis 11, we end up with a different year for the flood. The biblical story loses its time accuracy without this inclusion.

The Missing Piece

For the longest time, my numbers were off. The timeline I had created did not work out. Then I found the missing piece between Genesis 11 and Luke 3. There was a problem between Arphaxad and Shelah because Cainan was missing. Once I added Cainan, it all worked out. This is why studying the chronology of Scripture excites me!

With the addition of Cainan, Genesis 5 and Genesis 11 offer a complete genealogy from Adam to Abraham. Knowing their birth years and using the span of their lives, we can put together a complete timeline:

- Adam (4344 BC–3414 BC)

- Seth (4214 BC–3302 BC)

- Enosh (4109 BC–3204 BC)

- Kenan (4019 BC–3109 BC)

- Mahalalel (3949 BC–3054 BC)

- Jared (3884 BC–2922 BC)

- Enoch (3722 BC–3357 BC)

- Methuselah (3657 BC–2688 BC)

- Lamech (3470 BC–2693 BC)

- Noah (3288 BC–2338 BC)

- Shem (2786 BC–2186 BC)

- Arphaxad (2686 BC–2148 BC)

- Cainan (2551 BC–2091 BC)

- Shelah (2421 BC–1988 BC)

- Eber (2391 BC–1927 BC)

- Peleg (2357 BC–2118 BC)

- Reu (2327 BC–2088 BC)

- Serug (2295 BC–2065 BC)

- Nahor (2265 BC–2117 BC)

- Terah (2236 BC–2031 BC)

- Abraham (2166 BC–1991 BC).

Why is Cainan listed in Luke 3 but not in Genesis 11?

We know that Luke was a physician (Colossians 4:14), and he was clearly interested in details. A doctor needs to know meticulous details—for example, the difference between an artery and a vein and where they're located in the body. Otherwise, the physician can't do a proper job. Dr. Luke was paying attention to detail when he put his genealogy together.

When citing Old Testament Scriptures in his Gospel, Luke used the Septuagint, as did many other New Testament authors.[6] The Septuagint is the earliest existing Greek translation of what we consider the Old Testament.[7] At some point over the years, a scribe who was copying Genesis in its original Hebrew may have accidentally left Cainan out of Genesis 11. Luke, however, was working from an older, much-reviewed text that included Cainan, and he added that name to his genealogy of Christ to make sure there was no gap.

It is also because of the Septuagint that we're able to assign a date to Cainan. It tells us that Cainan's father, Arphaxad, was 135 years old when Cainan was born and that Cainan was 130 years old when his son Shelah was born.[8]

Although we might look at the omission of Cainan in Genesis 11 and consider it an error, it's important to remember that all Scripture is inspired by God (2 Timothy 3:16). God is ultimately sovereign over what the Bible includes and what is left out, as well as what's left out in one part of the Bible and added back in another. Deuteronomy 29:29 states, "The secret things belong to the LORD our God, but those things which are revealed belong to us and to our children forever, that we may do all the words of this law" (NKJV). God has His reasons for doing things the way He does, and we don't always understand them.

It's important to the serious Bible student that the line is unbroken from Adam to Abraham. Connecting Genesis 11 and Luke 3 reveals that the timeline is complete. It shows that God's story isn't missing any parts; He will work out His plan of salvation no matter what. God has given us all of the pieces, but as we've just seen, they might not all be found in one place.

Blessed Through Righteous Men

In Genesis 5, we see that Enoch was the only individual who was translated from earth to heaven without having to experience death. This happened because he "walked with God" (Genesis 5:22 NKJV), which I would define as living a holy life of loving obedience to the Lord. Enoch was a righteous man living in a world of unrighteous people, and because of that, God protected him from death.

The same was true of Noah. Because he chose to walk with God, living a holy life of loving obedience, God protected Noah and his family line and kept them from perishing in the flood like the rest of mankind. God truly watches over His own.

Looking at this line of people from Noah to Abraham, we see that God was working to create a holy people who would walk with Him in obedience. Before the flood, God's original mandate for mankind was being twisted and corrupted because people were working for their own glory and not for the glory of God.

After the floodwaters subsided and God had established a line of righteous men, He decided that instead of focusing on the mass of humanity, He would focus on one family and bless all mankind through them. With Abraham, the Lord God initiated a new path to righteousness: living by faith. The blessing of Abraham would apply to all who believe in the Name of the Lord.

The LORD had said to Abram, "Go from your country, your people and your father's household to the land I will show you. I will make you into a great nation, and I will bless you; I will make your name great, and you will be a blessing. I will bless those who bless you, and whoever curses you I will curse; and all peoples on earth will be blessed through you."
—Genesis 12:1–3

Before the flood, man was full of sin. After the flood, man still possessed a sin problem. The flood did not remove man's sin. The people between Noah and Abraham still sinned the same way we do today. If left to themselves, human beings do not live holy lives. They must truly have it in their hearts to walk by faith, not by sight, and to follow God wholeheartedly. The will of man must choose life over death.

In Abraham, God saw a man who was willing to be set apart for Him, a man who would "live by faith, not by sight" (2 Corinthians 5:7). Abraham left his homeland and went to a place he didn't know, the land of Canaan, trusting God to guide him by day and by night. He was willing to continue to worship God through good times and bad. He was willing to set up a new life with his wife and household, following God in an unfamiliar land.

Through the ages, the Lord God narrowed the scope of His great plan of salvation to focus on one Person: Jesus Christ, the Son of God. We see that God made mankind—Adam and Eve—and then narrowed His focus to Noah, then to Abraham, then to the Jews, and ultimately to Jesus Christ. Keep in mind that God narrowed His focus in response to obedience; He wasn't randomly picking and choosing favorites. Each step was intentional on the path to bringing forth the Messiah. Through the Messiah, Jesus Christ, God has blessed all mankind with the offer of salvation and forgiveness of sins.

God wants all men to live holy lives of loving obedience to Him. He wants us to love Him with all our hearts, souls, minds, and strength and to love our neighbors as ourselves (Luke 10:27). Through Jesus, we are able to do exactly that.

God's Plan Will Prevail

Though mankind has been sinful since creation, God always has had a plan to bring us into right standing with Him. Our heavenly Father knew exactly how to place people in that righteous line so that His will would be accomplished. Even though mankind is imperfect, messing up and failing to live holy lives, God still uses us to bring about His sovereign plan.

All of these dates, numbers, and names remind us that in the plan of God, people have significance. Biblical characters can be traced and tied to specific times in history. Truthfully, we don't need to know any of this information to be saved—that is Christ's work alone—but having this information helps us to see that God is involved in even the most minute details of our lives.

All the way back to Adam in 4344 BC, God's sovereign hand has been working out the details of people's lives. This reminds me that God is faithful. He does what He does perfectly, and we can trust Him. The God who interacted with Adam and Eve in the Garden of Eden is the same God who interacts with you and me right now. If God's plan can prevail despite the fall of mankind, how much more will it prevail for those who have been saved by grace through Jesus Christ!

Chapter Three Questions

Question: Why do you think that God wants us to study His Word? Why does He sometimes hide details or allow mysteries surrounding the Scriptures? How committed are you to searching out these things for yourself? Read and reflect on Proverbs 25:2.

_____

_____

_____

_____

_____

_____

_____

_____

_____

Question: Give examples from history and/or your own life of how God's plan always prevails, even in the face of human sin. Based on the promises from the New Testament, what is God's plan for you as a believer? What are some things that you believe may be part of His specific plan for you as an individual?

_____

_____

_____

_____

_____

_____

_____

_____

_____

_____

_____

_____

Action: Choose something from a biblical account that has never made sense to you. Start with the belief that the Bible is true and ask God to show you the veracity and reliability of His Word. Then spend time in serious study, using Bible study books and online resources, to come to a better understanding of the part of Scripture you do not yet understand.

Chapter Three Notes

CHAPTER FOUR

Abraham, Isaac, Jacob, and Joseph

In the Bible, there are four genealogies that are important to me and that form the pillars of my system of dating Scripture: Genesis 5, Genesis 11, Luke 3, and Matthew 1. Starting with the date of 966 BC from 1 Kings 6:1 and using the genealogies of Genesis 5 and 11 and Luke 3, I can date from Adam's birth to Abraham's death— from 4344 BC to 1991 BC. First Kings 6:1, with its date of 966 BC, is a pivotal verse in the dating system, as I mentioned earlier.

Many find it difficult to conceive of dating the lives of early prominent biblical characters, but I hope to show you that it is indeed possible to date biblical figures from Abraham to Jesus Christ. It takes a sufficient amount of time to be convinced of such study in the Word, but once the process is engrained, there is a lot of joy in realizing God that has left us a pathway through the Bible to provide proof of His sovereign activity.

When studying genealogies, we see a significant amount of overlap in the lives of the early patriarchs. As previously mentioned, their stories and experiences stood a greater chance of being passed down due to the overlapping generations. God did not leave Himself without a witness; hence, it is important to Him that we have these records.

Once I get beyond Abraham, Isaac, Jacob, and Joseph, however, it is impossible to date all of the individuals in the intervening periods accurately. The Bible simply doesn't give enough information about some individuals mentioned, and I'm sure that the Lord has His reasons for that, just as He has His reasons for giving us the information He does. My focus is purely on the line of Jesus Christ because that is what I want, a complete line of personalities and dates from Adam to Jesus. The Bible supplies us that information and does not disappoint.

From a Family to a Nation

As we get to Abraham, it's important to note that we are moving into a different period. Instead of working with the whole of humanity, God has narrowed His focus and chosen to work with one family. From this family, He will build a nation to walk with Him and live in holiness and obedience. He does this through the patriarchs of Abraham, Isaac, Jacob, and Joseph.

To date these individuals, we need to start again with the information in 1 Kings and work our way backward:

In the four hundred and eightieth year after the Israelites came out of Egypt, in the fourth year of Solomon's reign over Israel, in the month of Ziv, the second month, he began to build the temple of the LORD.

—1 Kings 6:1

The date of 1 Kings 6:1 is 966 BC, and I believe that it is good to memorize that date. To ensure that the date of 1 Kings 6:1 is secured through several other facts, allow me to list the facts so that you can better grasp them:[9]

- 966–959 BC: Solomon's Temple was constructed (1 Kings 6:1, 38).

- 853 BC: Assyrians fought the Aramean kings in the Battle of Qarqar in the sixth year of Shalmaneser III's reign.

- 853 BC: Ahab died from wounds in the Battle of Ramoth-Gilead (1 Kings 22:35).

- 841 BC: In the eighteenth year of Shalmaneser III's reign, he received tribute from Jehu, king of Israel.

- 841 BC: Jehu ascended the throne of Israel (1 Kings 22:51).

- June 15, 763 BC: The Assyrian eclipse, also known as the Bur-Sagale Eclipse, was a solar eclipse that helps fix dates for most of the Assyrian kings as recorded in the Assyrian eponym lists.

- 722 BC: The northern kingdom of Israel (nine

and a half tribes) was conquered by the Assyrians.

The events listed above help us to establish the date for 1 Kings 6:1. (See Appendix A for more information about using 1 Kings 6:1 to establish biblical dates.)

Returning to the text, if we add 480 years to 966 BC, we get 1446 BC for the date of the exodus. To be clear, this text informs us that the exodus occurred in 1446 BC, and 480 years after that, in 966 BC, construction began on Solomon's Temple.

The exodus of Israel out of Egypt lasted forty years (Numbers 14:34; Deuteronomy 1:3). The journey to the promised land should have been measured in days or weeks. Had Israel been an obedient nation and people of faith, their journey would have been significantly shorter. Because of their lack of faith in God and their disobedience, God allowed the journey to last forty hard years. There is a message in that for us all!

Immediately preceding the exodus, there was the sojourn, which was the length of time the Israelites lived in Egypt. Exodus 12:40–41 tells us, "Now the length of time the Israelite people lived in Egypt was 430 years. At the end of the 430 years, to the very day, all the LORD's divisions left Egypt." If we take the exodus (1446 BC) and add 430 years to it, we get a date of 1876 BC. Hence, we come to realize that the sojourn of Israel in the land of Egypt lasted from 1876 BC to 1446 BC.

Joseph was the one who initially went into Egypt. He later brought his father, Jacob, and his brothers and their households to Egypt and settled them there (Genesis 47:11–12). We can see Jacob's age and lifespan in Genesis 47:28: "Jacob lived in Egypt seventeen years, and the years of his life were a hundred and forty-seven."

Knowing how long Jacob lived in Egypt and how long he lived in total, we can calculate that he lived 130 years outside of Egypt. By adding 430 years to 1446 BC—the length of the sojourn to the date of the exodus—we get 1876 BC for the beginning of the sojourn. By subtracting the 17 years Jacob lived in Egypt from 1876 BC, we get 1859 BC as the year of Jacob's death. Putting all of these pieces of information together, we can say that the lifespan of Jacob was from 2006 BC to 1859 BC—147 years.

As we move from Adam to Jacob, we need to be at 1876 BC when Jacob was 130 years old. Thanks to the information Scripture provides, we can now date Joseph's life. Genesis 41:46 tells us, "Joseph was thirty years old when he entered the service of Pharaoh king of Egypt. And Joseph went out from Pharaoh's presence and traveled throughout Egypt." Joseph traveled throughout the land because, according to the visions he had, there would be seven years of plenty and seven years of famine (Genesis 41:29–30), and preparations needed to be made. The point here is that Joseph was thirty years old at the time.

When Joseph revealed himself to his brothers, he informed them that he would provide for them in Egypt during the five years of famine still to come (Genesis 45:9–11). When Jacob, who was 130 years old, arrived in Egypt, Joseph was 39. Seven years of plenty and two years of famine had passed since Joseph had entered the service of Pharaoh at age 30.

We know that Joseph lived 110 years (Genesis 50:26). If he was 39 when he was reunited with his father and brothers, this means that he lived 71 years afterward. The reunion took place in 1876 BC, which puts the year of Joseph's death at 1805 BC. It is now fully possible to date the lives of all four patriarchs. Knowing the dates for Abraham, Isaac, Jacob, and Joseph helps me to piece together the rest of the story:

- Abraham: 2166 BC–1991 BC (Genesis 11:26; 25:7)

- Isaac: 2066 BC–1886 BC (Genesis 21:2–5; 35:28)

- Jacob: 2006 BC–1859 BC (Genesis 25:26; 47:28)

- Joseph: 1915 BC–1805 BC (Genesis 41:46; 45:11; 47:28; 50:26)

- The Sojourn: 1876 BC–1446 BC (Exodus 12:40)

- The Exodus: 1446 BC–1406 BC (Deuteronomy 1:3).

Working Backward

By using the information found in 1 Kings 6:1 (see Appendix A), we're able to work backward to create the following timeline:

- 966 BC: We have established this as the date of 1 Kings 6:1.

- 1406 BC: The Israelites no longer had to wander in the wilderness. We know that there were forty years from the beginning of the exodus to the Israelites' entrance into the promised land because of Numbers 14:34.

- 1446 BC: The exodus began.

- 1876 BC: Jacob, his sons, and their households arrived in Egypt.

To find Isaac's lifespan, we have to start with Abraham and then work our way from Abraham to Jacob. As I have already established, Abraham lived from 2166 BC to 1991 BC. Genesis 25:7 tells us that "Abraham lived a hundred and seventy-five years." According to Genesis 21:5, he was 100 years old when Isaac was born. This means that Isaac was born in 2066 BC.

Scripture gives us some other information about Isaac. Genesis 35:28 tells us that he lived 180 years. Combining the information that the Bible provides for Abraham and Isaac, we're able to establish that Isaac was born in 2066 BC and died in 1886 BC.

Genesis 25:26 tells us that Isaac was sixty years old when his twin sons, Jacob and Esau, were born. We're more concerned about Jacob in this case because he was the patriarch through whom God would continue to carry out His plan of salvation. Jacob was born in 2006 BC and lived, as stated in Genesis 47:28, 147 years. This puts his year of death at 1859 BC.

Now, this is the point where I need to confirm whether I'm on the right track with my dates. If Jacob was the patriarch who led the Israelites into Egypt and began the sojourn, he would have needed to go to Egypt at some point in his life, and I need to be able to date that. This is where Genesis 47:28, which provides all of that information, is vitally important in its connection to 1 Kings 6:1.

Working through the math, Jacob would need to be 130 years old when he arrived in Egypt, as he lived in Egypt for seventeen years and lived a total of 147 years (Genesis 47:28). Taking 17 years away from his date of death, 1859 BC, gives us 1876 BC, the start of the sojourn in Egypt. When all of the information I have presented falls into place, the date of 966 BC for 1 Kings 6:1 is confirmed. A correct date for 1 Kings 6:1 enables us to be accurate with a lot of other biblical dates.

The Favored Son

From Jacob, we turn to Joseph, whose life we can date as 1915 BC to 1805 BC. The Bible makes it clear that Joseph was Jacob's favorite son:

> Now Israel loved Joseph more than any of his other sons, because he had been born to him in his old age; and he made an ornate robe for him.
>
> **—Genesis 37:3**

Drawing upon information previously presented, if you

do the math, you'll notice that Jacob was 91 when he had Joseph through his wife Rachel. (Remember, when Jacob was reunited with Joseph in Egypt, he was 130 years old, and Joseph was 39.) Jacob surely recalled how his father, Isaac, had been born to his grandfather, Abraham, when the latter was 100 years old. Esau and Jacob were born when Isaac was 60.

Jacob must have realized the significance of the promised son coming in the father's old age, and he would have recognized that God's promises of His faithfulness to His people would come through his son Joseph. Having this context helps us to understand why Joseph was the favorite son, why his father made him a special robe, and why Joseph's brothers were so jealous of him (Genesis 37:3–4). It gets to the heart of the theology of the story.

Going back to the genealogy in Genesis 11, we see that the patriarchs in Shem's line were in their thirties when their sons were born. Jacob, on the other hand, was in his nineties, and Abraham was 100. It would have been quite dramatic for Jacob to realize that God's favor was resting on Joseph's life because Joseph was born much later than what was considered normal at that time.

Jacob was Rachel's firstborn son. Though Scripture doesn't tell us anything about how old Rachel was when Joseph was born, it was unlikely that she was a young woman in her natural childbearing years. She was advancing in age. But as He did with Sarah, God made sure that Rachel would have the promised son:

Then God remembered Rachel; he listened to her and enabled her to conceive. She became pregnant and gave birth to a son and said, "God has taken away my disgrace." She named him Joseph, and said, "May the LORD add to me another son."

—Genesis 30:22–24

God knew that Joseph's brothers, in their jealousy, would sell him to the Ishmaelites, who would sell him into slavery in Egypt (Genesis 37:28). But He also knew that Joseph would become second-in-command to Pharaoh and save the Israelite nation from starvation during a seven-year drought. In a foreshadowing of the salvation that would ultimately come through Christ Jesus, God used the favored son to rescue His people.

God does great, seemingly impossible things in people's lives. The Bible is full of examples in which it should not have been possible for something to happen, "but with God all things are possible" (Matthew 19:26). Working with numbers, which do not lie, helps support the notion that our God is a miracle-working God.

God at Work

It's important to understand that God worked His divine plan through Abraham's line. After all, Abraham was the one to whom He made the promise:

"I will surely bless you and make your descendants as numerous as the stars in the sky and as the sand on the seashore. Your descendants will take possession of the cities of their enemies, and through your offspring all nations on earth will be blessed, because you have obeyed me."

—Genesis 22:17–18

From Abraham, God continued to work out the fulfillment of this promise through Isaac and Jacob. It's Jacob's life, however, that ties into that key verse of 1 Kings 6:1 and makes it possible for the rest of the numbers involving these patriarchs to come together.

It's not by happenstance that the numbers come together; it's by the divine plan of God. He wants us to understand that He is working it out. He is a very exact and specific God. He does not fail. We may not understand His ways, but what He has chosen to give us in Scripture is absolutely important.

In that vein, Genesis is a crucial book to understand. God does not give us the necessary information to date the lifespans of many of the people mentioned in that book. However, He does devote numerous chapters to the lives of Abraham, Isaac, Jacob, and Joseph so that we can recognize the importance of their lives to the divine plan of God.

Theologically, dates remind us that God is real, and they bring the Bible closer to home. Jacob was alive just 4,000 years ago! The story of God working out our redemption is not as long ago as we might think.

If God included information in His Word that enables us to date the lives of these patriarchs, we can be confident that He is concerned with the times and dates of our lives as well. I am comforted to know that God knows my beginning and my end. He will not leave me or forsake me (Deuteronomy 31:6).

Right Place, Right Time

Abraham, Isaac, Jacob, and Joseph represent the founding of the great nation of Israel. They show us the movement of God in history and how God will bring His people to a place of understanding where they live by faith in Him.

Theologically speaking, Abraham was the father of the faithful because he "believed the LORD, and he credited it to him as righteousness" (Genesis 15:6). Abraham is mentioned several times in the "hall of faith" in Hebrews 11.

I hang a great deal of theology on my favorite verse from Hebrews 11:

> *By faith Abraham, when called to go to a place he would later receive as his inheritance, obeyed and went, even though he did not know where he was going.*
> **—Hebrews 11:8**

God calls each of us, and when He does, it's important to obey. When we obey, He takes us to places we may never have thought about going on our own. Like Abraham, we follow God by faith, not knowing where we're going. We follow Him because we know that He is giving us a better inheritance than we can possibly make for ourselves.

Abraham's son Isaac was the son promised by God, but Isaac then had twin sons, Jacob and Esau. Jacob was chosen by God, but Esau was not (Malachi 1:2–3). Though a nation was born from each brother—Esau being the father of the Edomites and Jacob being the father of the

Israelites—it was Jacob and his lineage who were counted among the faithful. Even within Jacob's lineage, we see that some individuals played a bigger part in God's plan than others.

God moved through this nation of people to bring about His plan. Our lives are similar to theirs. We all have family, and we all know that some family members are chosen by God to do different or bigger things than other family members. We must learn that when God calls us to go with Him, we are to obey Him immediately and let Him use our lives however He wants to use them for His glory.

There is no way to predict all the ways God will lead us throughout our lives. There will be turns and obstacles, straight paths and winding roads. Such is the adventure of faith.

Studying the lives of Abraham, Isaac, Jacob, and Joseph helps us to see how God puts people in the right places at the right times to accomplish His will. Having dates for their lives transforms their stories from black and white to color. As we continue to move through the Bible, we'll see how God brought Jesus into the world at exactly the right time.

When God makes a promise, He keeps it. Having these important dates helps us to see that His plan is right on schedule—heaven's schedule—and lines up with history. God works in His own perfect time.

Chapter Four Questions

Question: Isaac, Jacob, and Joseph were all sons of their fathers' old age. Describe a time in your own life (or that of someone you know) when it seemed that God had waited until it was too late to fulfill His promise, yet He came through in a way that brought even greater glory to Himself and made the fulfillment miraculous and memorable.

_____

_____

_____

_____

_____

_____

_____

_____

_____

_____

Question: In what ways have you seen God's care over the little details of your life? What scriptures support this concept that He is concerned with the very smallest details of each person's life?

_____

_____

_____

_____

_____

_____

_____

_____

_____

_____

_____

Action: How has someone else's step of faith helped to fulfill God's plan in your own life? Take time this week to thank a friend or mentor who has impacted you by willingly obeying God even without knowing His plan. How does this person's example encourage you to follow God in faith? What step of faith has He put on your heart?

Chapter Four Notes

_____

_____

_____

_____

_____

_____

_____

_____

_____

_____

_____

_____

_____

_____

_____

_____

_____

_____

_____

_____

_____

_____

CHAPTER FIVE

United Monarchy: Saul to Solomon

Before we move on from the patriarchs and dig into the next era of biblical history, it's important to note that the promise of Abraham was repeated to Isaac, his son, and to Jacob, his grandson, but it wasn't repeated to Joseph, his great-grandson. Why not Joseph?

I believe it is because Joseph was sold into slavery at the age of 17, became an Egyptian citizen and the second-most-powerful man in the country, and spent most of his life as an Egyptian, rather than as an Israelite. God perfectly knew all of this in advance, and that's why the promise of Abraham was not shared by Joseph and why he is not in the line that stretches from Adam to Jesus. (See Matthew 1 and Luke 3.)

Instead of Joseph, there is Judah, son of Jacob, in the genealogical line. Since Joseph's life occupies such a large portion of Genesis—chapters 37 to 50—I have to believe that the reason Joseph is not included in the official lineage is because he was considered a foreigner.

Moses, Joshua, and the Judges

From Joseph, we move on to the next great figure in the faith, a one-of-a-kind Israelite with a powerful position in Egypt: Moses. Although his early life included being raised as the adopted son of Pharaoh's daughter, Moses would eventually play a significant role in Israel's history in the period leading up to the kings. He was God's chosen vessel to lead the Israelites out of slavery in Egypt. He would also be the one to receive the law of God directly from God's hand on Mount Sinai. This law would become the identifying object of the Jews as the people of God.

The Israelites prospered in Egypt for seventy-one years due to Joseph's leadership and protection, but eventually "there arose a new king over Egypt, who did not know Joseph" (Exodus 1:8 NKJV). This king thought that the Israelites had become too numerous and feared that they might rebel, so he subjected them to forced labor to keep them under control (Exodus 1:9–14).

We can date the life of Moses because we know that the Israelites' sojourn in Egypt, as we have previously worked out, lasted from 1876 BC to 1446 BC. The exodus of Israel occurred in 1446 BC, followed by a forty-year period of wandering in the wilderness that ended in 1406 BC.

Scripture tells us that "Moses was eighty years old and Aaron eighty-three when they spoke to Pharaoh" (Exodus 7:7). Deuteronomy 34:7 states, "Moses was a hundred and twenty years old when he died, yet his eyes were not weak nor his strength gone." Moses died just before the children of Israel entered the promised land. With all of this information, we can date the life of Moses as being from 1526 BC to 1406 BC. His life was divided very neatly into three sections. He spent forty years in Egypt, forty years in Midian, and forty years leading the children of Israel out of Egypt and through the wilderness.

Joshua is a little trickier for us to date. We know that he became the leader of Israel in 1406 BC, following the death of Moses. He led the nation of Israel for about twenty years, from 1406 BC to 1386 BC, as they conquered foreign kings and territories within the promised land.

I derive this twenty-year period for Joshua's leadership from the following scripture:

> The God of the people of Israel chose our ancestors; he made the people prosper during their stay in Egypt; with mighty power he led them out of that country; for about forty years he endured their conduct in the wilderness; and he overthrew seven nations in Canaan, giving their land to his people as their inheritance. All this took about 450 years.
> **—Acts 13:17–20a**

Exodus 12:40, as you may remember, tells us that the Israelites lived in Egypt for 430 years, so we can subtract that from the 450 years referenced in Acts 13:20 to find out that Joshua led the Israelites for twenty years.

Joshua's leadership was followed by the period of the judges, which lasted about 334 years. I arrive at this number by doing simple math with information in 1 Kings 6:1 and taking into consideration the dates of the sojourn in Egypt, the exodus, and the lives of Moses and Joshua. The period of the judges was from the end of Joshua's leadership in 1386 BC to 1052 BC.

The period of the judges is difficult to calculate because even though the book of Judges includes the length of the reigns of many of the judges, some reigns overlapped—meaning that there may have been multiple judges reigning at the same time in different parts of Israel.

It is difficult to tell when there was a single judge reigning and when there were co-judges reigning simultaneously. But by doing the math and working backward from 1 Kings 6:1, we're able to come up with 334 years as a fairly solid estimate.

Israel's First Earthly King

The book of Judges concludes with the statement: "In those days there was no king in Israel; everyone did what was right in his own eyes" (Judges 21:25 NKJV). It wasn't long, however, before the Israelites insisted on having a king to rule them. The elders approached Samuel, the last of the judges, and presented their request:

> They said to him, "You are old, and your sons do not follow your ways; now appoint a king to lead us, such as all the other nations have."
>
> **—1 Samuel 8:5**

God did not intend for Israel to be ruled by a human king. He wanted to be their King of choice. He agreed to their request, but only after warning them about the rights an earthly king would claim: he would conscript their sons into the military, take their daughters to work in the palace, and take the best of their agricultural produce and livestock (1 Samuel 8:10–18).

Following the instructions given by God, Samuel anointed Saul, of the tribe of Benjamin, as king over Israel (1 Samuel 10) in 1052 BC. Saul was the first of three kings who reigned over all twelve tribes of Israel in a period known as the united monarchy. In an interesting parallel to Moses' life, which can be divided into three phases of forty years each, each of the three kings in this period reigned for about forty years.

Saul was born in 1082 BC and died in 1010 BC, giving him a lifespan of seventy-two years. First Samuel 13:1 tells us, "Saul was thirty years old when he became king, and he reigned over Israel forty-two years."

Acts 13:21 seems to round that number a bit, stating that Saul ruled for forty years. I use the number from 1 Samuel 13:1 since it's more precise. If Saul was thirty years old when he became king and 72 when he died, the math certainly indicates that he reigned for forty-two years. This puts the dates for Saul's reign at 1052 BC–1010 BC.

David and Solomon

After the death of Saul in 1010 BC, David took the throne. He was a man after God's heart (1 Samuel 13:14), and his rich relationship with the Lord provided material for nearly half of the Psalms. It is also through David's line that Jesus Christ, the promised Messiah, came.

First Kings 2:11 states that David "reigned forty years over Israel—seven years in Hebron and thirty-three in Jerusalem." Second Samuel 5:4 provides a little more information, adding that "David was thirty years old when he became king." This means that David was seventy years old when he died, which means that he lived from 1040 BC to 970 BC.

Some people might think that David lived to be a really old man, but he did not. Compared to Moses, whom God allowed to live to the 120-year maximum, David lived only about half as long. Even today, seventy years isn't considered a long life. This prayer of Moses comes to mind when I consider the years God gives us: "Our days may come to seventy years, or eighty, if our strength endures; yet the best of them are but trouble and sorrow, for they quickly pass, and we fly away" (Psalm 90:10).

Like Saul, David also reigned for forty years. God loves consistency! David's reign lasted from 1010 BC to 970 BC. It is a rich story.

Next is Solomon, who was born in 999 BC and died in 930 BC, giving him a lifespan of sixty-nine years. We see a pattern emerging. Saul lived for seventy-two years, David lived for seventy years, Solomon lived for sixty-nine years, and each of them reigned for forty years. Through these three kings, God worked to bring peace and stability to the nation of Israel.

Solomon was twenty-nine years old when he began to reign over Israel, while his father was still alive (1 Kings

1:43–2:12). Does this represent a brief period of co-regency? Maybe. We can date Solomon's solo reign as being from 970 BC to 931 BC. My understanding of Scripture indicates that Solomon was a co-regent with his father for less than a year, which could make his reign from 971 BC to 931 BC.

Solomon was the first king to use the ascension-year method of dating a king's reign. Using this method means that the first year of a king's reign would be counted as year zero, not year one. As such, the ascension year counts toward the reign of the king's predecessor—in this case, Solomon's father, David. Even though Solomon took the throne in 971 BC, his reign didn't officially begin until 970 BC.

A date of 970 BC works very well as the beginning of Solomon's reign because of the information we have already presented surrounding the date in 1 Kings 6:1. The king began to build the temple in the fourth year of his reign, which matches up with our date of 966 BC.

According to Edwin R. Thiele, dating of a king's reign began in the month of Tishri of his ascension year.[10] Tishri (September–October) is the first month of the Jewish civil year and the seventh month of the religious year, which begins in Nisan (March–April). Having a calendar year and a religious year is not unheard of. I liken this to corporations having a fiscal year that is on a different schedule from the calendar year. This would be similar to a company starting their fiscal year in June rather than January.

This is important to keep in mind as we look at Scripture that provides additional information regarding the construction of the temple:

> *The foundation of the LORD's Temple was laid in midspring,
> in the month of Ziv, during the fourth year of Solomon's
> reign. The entire building was completed in every detail by
> midautumn, in the month of Bul, during the eleventh year of
> his reign. So it took seven years to build the Temple.*
>
> **—1 Kings 6:37–38** (NLT)

Some biblical versions of this story say that it took seven and a half years. Let me clear this up. Look again at the NLT version above. It states that the building of the temple went from mid-spring of the fourth year to mid-autumn of the eleventh year. This would be seven Nisans plus six months more. I presented the NLT version here for you to see clearly that it took seven and a half years to complete, but to say seven years is definitely acceptable.

After the united monarchy split into the northern kingdom of Israel and the southern kingdom of Judah, the kings of Judah continued to follow the precedent Solomon had set and used the ascension-year method of dating their reigns. The kings of Israel, however, did not use this method, meaning that the dates of their reigns began as soon as they took the throne. It's helpful to remember this fact as you attempt to date various kings. The kings of Israel did not date the same way the kings of Judah dated, making it rather confusing.

When we put those two systems of dating together and we understand where each king was ruling, we end up with a beautiful calendar in which all of the dates and numbers work. This process is exactly what Thiele does in his book *The Mysterious Numbers of the Hebrew Kings.*[11] His reconstruction of the period of the kings of Judah and Israel supports the date for 1 Kings 6:1 as being 966 BC, based on what we know about Solomon and the ascension-year method of dating he used. From there, we can extrapolate the chronology of Scripture.

A Time of Stability and Unity

The period of the united monarchy revealed that God was concerned about the leadership of the nation of Israel and the unity of the nation. He gave the three kings—Saul, David, and Solomon—opportunities to fix their mistakes for the sake of the unity of the kingdom and the good of the people. Through these fallible, sin-prone leaders, God showed His people that it would take more than a human king to transform them into the righteous people He wanted them to be.

Before the united monarchy and its 120-year period of consistent, forty-year reigns, the judges ruled over Israel for various lengths of time—anywhere from several months to several decades. The period of the judges was chaotic and unpredictable, and the period of the kings brought much-needed stability. In both cases, the people needed more than human leadership; they needed to reach out to God Himself.

Forty is one of those numbers that is repeated throughout Scripture. It rained for forty days and forty nights without stopping in Noah's day; the Israelites spent forty years in the desert following their exodus from Egypt; Moses led Israel for forty years and was on Mount Sinai for forty days; Jesus fasted for forty days and nights in the wilderness; and, as we have calculated, the kings of the united monarchy reigned for forty years each. From information I have presented, forty years represents approximately one hour of God's time. Although minutes and seconds are important, an hour of time represents a moment with God.

I do not want to make too much out of this point, but I think it is worth noting. Revelation 18:10 says, "For in one hour your judgment has come" (NKJV). The same text in the NLT states, "In a single moment God's judgment came on you." It definitely is a matter of translation, but we can understand that what appear to be long periods of time to us make up only moments of time for God. The Almighty views time differently from how we see it.

From the exodus to the united monarchy, the dwelling place of God was in a tabernacle, which can be described as a mobile tent. In the united monarchy, during the reign of Solomon, the construction of God's temple occurred in Jerusalem. Instead of God's presence being housed within the tabernacle, which was mobile, He established His presence among the people in a permanent, immovable structure. This, too, was an indication that Israel was entering a more stable period in history with God.

God chose Saul to be the first human king of Israel in response to the request of the people, as Saul fit the requirements for kingship in their eyes. He was handsome and tall (1 Samuel 9:2) and a strong military leader (1 Samuel 11). Saul soon went astray, however, and disqualified himself as king by failing to follow God's commands.

In response, God raised up David to succeed Saul. This time, God chose a king who fit His requirements for kingship: "a man after his own heart" (1 Samuel 13:14; 1 Samuel 16:7). God desired to show His favor to His people by blessing them with a king after His own heart, which is why He promised David that his family would rule forever: "Your house and your kingdom will endure forever before me; your throne will be established forever" (2 Samuel 7:16).

The promise to David was ultimately fulfilled in Jesus Christ, the Son of God, who was a descendant of the house of David. The genealogies we have been examining point out this fact. There is a direct line from Abraham to David to Jesus.

During the period of the united monarchy, Israel flourished. By the time Solomon took the throne, there was peace in the land, making it possible for him to build God's temple. Though David desired to build the temple, God did not allow him to do so because of the many wars he had fought and all of the blood he had shed (1 Chronicles 22:7–8). David's life consisted of seventy years of war, while Solomon's life consisted of sixty-nine years of peace.

It amazes me that God likes to work in nice, neat time frames under just the right conditions. He set up the united monarchy for His people, and under Solomon there was peace in the kingdom. Righteousness should have flourished. Why didn't it? Man would mess it up, thus requiring the Messiah to come and set things right.

Romans 14:17 states, "For the kingdom of God is not a matter of eating and drinking, but of righteousness, peace and joy in the Holy Spirit." In those neatly constructed moments of our lives when peace abides and joy splashes us, the righteousness of God becomes real, almost palpable. It's in those moments that we can sense the perfection of God's timing.

God Does Not Change

The God of order who so carefully orchestrated the united monarchy is the same God we worship today. He is the same God who is described throughout Scripture:

> Rend your heart and not your garments. Return to the LORD your God, for he is gracious and compassionate, slow to anger and abounding in love, and he relents from sending calamity.
>
> **—Joel 2:13**

These four qualities of God—His graciousness, His compassion, His slowness to anger, and His abundant love—appear seven times in the Old Testament (Exodus 34:6; Nehemiah 9:17; Psalm 86:15; Psalm 103:8; Psalm 145:8; Jonah 4:2). With that much repetition, we can be confident that He wants us to understand these aspects of His character.

Similarly, the chronology of Scripture reveals that God desires order in our lives. He wants us to do things in an orderly way. He gives us opportunities to make our choices, and He gives us time to correct our mistakes and get back on the right path. But as we saw with Saul, if we are not for God, He will ultimately find someone who is.

Saul rejected the opportunities God gave him to repent and turn back to Him, so God replaced him with David. David sinned against God by sleeping with Bathsheba and then murdering her husband (2 Samuel 11), but he took the opportunity that God gave him to repent and return to Him (2 Samuel 12).

God still disciplined David. The son he conceived in adultery with Bathsheba died, and he had to live with that scar on his heart for the rest of his life (2 Samuel 12:13–23). We, too, may have scars that we have to live with due to God's discipline for our disobedience, but we still need to move forward, playing our roles in God's plan.

God can still use us in our brokenness. He is not concerned with us being broken as much as He is concerned with us being broken open. If an egg breaks, you can't use it. But if an egg is broken open, you can use it. Similarly, when our lives are broken open, God can use us in mighty ways.

We want to make sure that we're living for God so that when He wants to use us for His good and glory, He can. I think that Solomon got the benefit of the doubt because his father was a righteous man. David found favor with God; therefore, his children found favor.

Likewise, if we walk with God and glorify Him through our loving obedience, His favor will rest not only on us, but also on our children (Exodus 20:6). They will reap blessings that God started with us, which will be revealed as God continues to work in His orderly ways.

We may not rule a nation like the kings of the united monarchy, but we are kings and queens over our lives and the spheres where we exist. We must choose whether we will allow God to use us for His good and glory. Over time, He will raise up the righteous and use them and their progeny to build His kingdom on earth.

If God could promise David that a member of his family would always sit on the throne of Israel, ultimately culminating in the coming Messiah, we can rest assured that God is faithful and cannot lie. He will do what He says He will do. The God of Abraham, Isaac, and Jacob, who was also the God of David, is the same faithful God to you and me.

WORKBOOK

Chapter Five Questions

Question: Look at the four qualities of God's nature that are repeated seven times in the Old Testament: graciousness, compassion, slowness to anger, and abundant love. Are these the ways that you normally think about God and describe Him to others? Are these qualities increasing in your own life as you continue to become more like Him?

_____

_____

Question: When you become aware of sin in your life, are you quick to take the opportunity to repent and make things right, or do you risk running the clock out on God's forbearance? What are some areas where you have been broken open, and how can these places of brokenness become places of great usefulness for the Lord?

_____

_____

_____

_____

_____

_____

_____

_____

_____

_____

_____

Action: God is a God of order. Is your life characterized by order or chaos? Evaluate the orderliness of the following aspects of your life:

- Your physical surroundings (home, office, car)
- Your time management
- Your physical health and habits
- Your spiritual life and growth.

Set a practical goal in each of these areas to increase the order and cut the chaos, and begin taking action on your goals this week.

Chapter Five Notes

CHAPTER SIX

Divided Kingdom: Rehoboam to Zedekiah

The united monarchy was a glorious period in the life of the nation Israel. Although the kingdom had its share of problems, for 120 years the people of God were one, under one leader—first Saul, then David, and then Solomon. But the desires of men have an uncanny way of messing up a good thing. Even leaders go awry. Solomon was succeeded as king by his son Rehoboam. However, the kingdom became divided by rebellion soon after Solomon's death, and the united monarchy drew to a close (1 Kings 12). We now enter the period of the divided kingdom.

With the people of Israel splitting their affections, Rehoboam was made king over the tribes of Judah and Benjamin, which became the southern kingdom of Judah, while Jeroboam was crowned king of the remaining ten tribes, which became the northern kingdom of Israel. Rehoboam reigned over Judah from 931 BC to 910 BC, and

Jeroboam reigned over Israel from 931 BC to 913 BC.

It would not be long—according to God's perspective of time—before both kingdoms would fall subservient to foreign invaders: Israel to Assyria and Judah to Babylon.

Important Dates for the Divided Kingdom

The Battle of Qarqar took place in 853 BC on the Orontes River in the sixth year of the reign of King Shalmaneser III of Assyria.[12] In this battle, the Assyrians fought against the Syrians and the Israelites. This is an important date in history that will help us to date the events of the divided kingdom period. The Assyrian eponym lists dates for the kings of Assyria with precision.

Ahab, the king of Israel, supplied Ben-Hadad, the king of Syria, with 2,000 chariots and 10,000 men to halt the advance of Shalmaneser III. This intervention later caused Assyria to make advances against Israel. Shortly thereafter, in 853 BC, fighting alongside Jehoshaphat king of Judah, Ahab died from wounds sustained in the Battle at Ramoth-Gilead, as recorded in Scripture:

> All day long the battle raged, and the king was propped up in his chariot facing the Arameans. The blood from his wound ran onto the floor of the chariot, and that evening he died.
>
> —*1 Kings 22:35*

From Ahab's death in 853 BC, we can supply other dates for kings during the divided kingdom.

In the eighteenth year of the reign of Shalmaneser III,

841 BC, he received a tribute from the king of Israel. At this point, Jehu was king of Israel, having ascended the throne in 831 BC.

We can date the reigns of the kings of Israel and Judah because we have the dates for the reigns of the Assyrian kings. The dates of Assyrian kings can be determined accurately because of an eclipse that took place on June 13, 763 BC, and information has been collected in what are known as the Assyrian eponym lists.[13]

Another extrabiblical date that helps us in dating the events of the divided kingdom period and adds color to the lives of these kings is 722 BC, the date when the northern kingdom of Israel was conquered by the Assyrians and the people were carried into captivity.[14]

We also know that in 701 BC (another hard date), King Sennacherib of Assyria set siege against the southern kingdom of Judah,[15] which enables us to date this verse:

In the fourteenth year of King Hezekiah's reign, Sennacherib king of Assyria attacked all the fortified cities of Judah and captured them.
—2 Kings 18:13

And of course, the date of 966 BC for the beginning of the construction of the temple continues to be an important date as well—the key date that helps us to establish the timeline of Scripture.

Judah Under Siege

After the northern kingdom of Israel fell to the

Assyrians in 722 BC, the southern kingdom of Judah began to suffer attacks from Babylon. King Nebuchadnezzar of Babylon attacked Jerusalem in 605 BC, 597 BC, and 586 BC—a total of three times.[16]

In 586 BC, the Babylonians set Jerusalem on fire and destroyed the temple.[17] Just as the people of Israel were carried into captivity by the Assyrians, the people of Judah were carried into captivity by the Babylonians. God vacated His temple in Jerusalem; His presence departed.

The first deportation to Babylon took place in 605 BC:[18]

In the third year of the reign of Jehoiakim king of Judah, Nebuchadnezzar king of Babylon came to Jerusalem and besieged it. And the Lord delivered Jehoiakim king of Judah into his hand, along with some of the articles from the temple of God. These he carried off to the temple of his god in Babylonia and put in the treasure house of his god.

Then the king ordered Ashpenaz, chief of his court officials, to bring into the king's service some of the Israelites from the royal family and the nobility—young men without any physical defect, handsome, showing aptitude for every kind of learning, well informed, quick to understand, and qualified to serve in the king's palace. He was to teach them the language and literature of the Babylonians.

—Daniel 1:1–4

Daniel and his three friends, Hananiah, Mishael, and Azariah—perhaps better known by their Babylonian names of Shadrach, Meshach, and Abednego—were part of the first deportation (Daniel 1:6–7). This helps us to date the events in the first part of the book of Daniel to

605 BC.

The second deportation took place in 597 BC:[19]

> *At that time the officers of Nebuchadnezzar king of Babylon advanced on Jerusalem and laid siege to it, and Nebuchadnezzar himself came up to the city while his officers were besieging it. Jehoiachin king of Judah, his mother, his attendants, his nobles and his officials all surrendered to him.*
>
> *In the eighth year of the reign of the king of Babylon, he took Jehoiachin prisoner. As the LORD had declared, Nebuchadnezzar removed the treasures from the temple of the LORD and from the royal palace, and cut up the gold articles that Solomon king of Israel had made for the temple of the LORD. He carried all Jerusalem into exile: all the officers and fighting men, and all the skilled workers and artisans—a total of ten thousand. Only the poorest people of the land were left.*
>
> **—2 Kings 24:10–14**

Ezekiel was part of this second deportation (Ezekiel 1:1–3), which helps us to date the events at the beginning of his book to around 597 BC.

The third and final deportation took place in 586 BC.[20] By this time, only a small group of people remained, along with Zedekiah, the last king of Judah:

> *So in the ninth year of Zedekiah's reign, on the tenth day of the tenth month, Nebuchadnezzar king of Babylon marched against Jerusalem with his whole army. He encamped outside the city and built siege works all around it. The city was kept under siege until the eleventh year of King Zedekiah.*
>
> **—2 Kings 25:1–2**

Finally, the Babylonians destroyed the temple and carried the remaining inhabitants of Jerusalem into exile:

> On the seventh day of the fifth month, in the nineteenth year of Nebuchadnezzar king of Babylon, Nebuzaradan commander of the imperial guard, an official of the king of Babylon, came to Jerusalem. He set fire to the temple of the LORD, the royal palace and all the houses of Jerusalem. Every important building he burned down. The whole Babylonian army under the commander of the imperial guard broke down the walls around Jerusalem. Nebuzaradan the commander of the guard carried into exile the people who remained in the city, along with the rest of the populace and those who had deserted to the king of Babylon. But the commander left behind some of the poorest people of the land to work the vineyards and fields.
>
> **—2 Kings 25:8–12**

Solomon's Temple was destroyed on August 14, 586 BC, and other important buildings in Jerusalem were burned down.[21]

When we look for God's orderliness in these dates and scriptures, we see that Nebuchadnezzar came against Jerusalem three times. The people were deported to Babylon in three waves. When the captivity was over, the people returned to rebuild and repopulate Jerusalem in three waves. God is consistent. As the people went, so would they return.

The Return to Jerusalem

In 539 BC, Babylon was overthrown by Persia, and in 538 BC, King Cyrus of Persia issued a decree to repopulate Jerusalem and rebuild the temple:[22]

> *In the first year of Cyrus king of Persia, in order to fulfill the word of the LORD spoken by Jeremiah, the LORD moved the heart of Cyrus king of Persia to make a proclamation throughout his realm and also to put it in writing:*
>
> *"This is what Cyrus king of Persia says:*
>
> *"'The LORD, the God of heaven, has given me all the kingdoms of the earth and he has appointed me to build a temple for him at Jerusalem in Judah. Any of his people among you may go up, and may the LORD their God be with them.'"*
>
> **—2 Chronicles 36:22–23**

This decree was issued forty-eight years after the First Temple was destroyed, which means that roughly a generation had passed. This number is also important because it's very close to the Year of Jubilee.

In Leviticus 25, God commanded His people to give the land a year of sabbath rest every seventh year. During that year, they were not to sow or reap in their fields or prune or harvest in their vineyards. After seven sabbath years came the Year of Jubilee:

> *"Count off seven sabbath years—seven times seven years— so that the seven sabbath years amount to a period of forty-nine years. Then have the trumpet sounded everywhere on the tenth day of the seventh month; on the Day of Atonement sound the trumpet throughout your land. Consecrate the fiftieth year and proclaim liberty throughout the land to*

> *all its inhabitants. It shall be a jubilee for you; each of you*
> *is to return to your family property and to your own clan."*
> **—Leviticus 25:8–10**

As I see it, God waited one Jubilee to restore His people and return them to the land He had given them. It's an insight easy to miss if we're not taking note of numbers and dates.

Three Waves of Returnees

Just as Nebuchadnezzar deported the people of Judah in three waves, there were three waves of people that returned to Jerusalem following Cyrus's decree. The first wave left Babylon in 538 BC and was led by Zerubbabel, Sheshbazzar, and Joshua (Ezra 1–6).[23] The group numbered close to 50,000 people (Ezra 2:64–65). They were the ones who started rebuilding the temple.

Construction on the Second Temple, which is often credited to King Darius (Ezra 6:15), soon came to a halt due to opposition from the surrounding peoples. The work was paused for almost sixteen years, but it resumed in 520 BC, and the temple was completed in 515 BC.[24]

This first group likely would have contained many people who were exiled from Jerusalem, who still remembered what the city had been like and longed to see both city and temple restored to their former glory. There probably would have been children and grandchildren in this group as well.

The second wave of returnees from Babylon in 458 BC[25] were led by Ezra (Ezra 7). This group numbered fewer than 2,000.[26] Looking at the years of departure for the first two groups of returnees, we see that the second group left Babylon eighty years after the first group. That's almost double the amount of time that the people of Judah spent in exile.

If we were to spend eighty years living in a different land, we would become so indoctrinated into the lifestyle of that country and those people that we might not want to return to the land we once called home. That's what seems to have happened to God's people by Ezra's time, and it explains why the second wave of returnees was so much smaller than the first.

Doing the math, more than 120 years had passed since the last exiles were deported from Jerusalem to Babylon. Why would any remaining Israelites in Babylon return to Jerusalem when Babylon was truly all they knew?

Ezra wanted to go back to Israel and was willing to lead others. Ezra 7:10 seems to hold the key: "For Ezra had devoted himself to the study and observance of the Law of the LORD, and to teaching its decrees and laws in Israel." His awareness of God was fueling his desire to worship God in the homeland.

He was aware that solid spiritual teaching was needed in Jerusalem, especially since the temple had been rebuilt. So, with God's gracious hand on him and the support of King Artaxerxes of Persia, he set out for Jerusalem to teach God's ways to His people.

Many of the Israelites who returned during the first wave in 538 BC had likely died, since people weren't living past 120 years of age at this point in history. This made the need for a firm spiritual foundation even more urgent.

The people of Israel needed the spiritual infusion that Ezra would provide.

The people who were returning to Jerusalem with Ezra were likely doing so because they wanted to leave behind the idolatry of Babylon and devote themselves to God wholeheartedly. Ezra 7:7 tells us that this group included "priests, Levites, musicians, gatekeepers and temple servants." Since the temple had been rebuilt, they were likely eager to serve as their ancestors did.

This group of 2,000 was a fresh group, and it was a fresh, new time for them to go to Jerusalem. What an incredible testimony that after more than 120 years in a foreign land where God was not worshiped, there was still a remnant among His people who were seeking Him.

The third and final group of returnees numbered nearly 50,000 people in total and left Babylon in 444 BC.[27] They were led by Nehemiah (Nehemiah 2). This final group departed Babylon nearly 150 years after the first exiles had arrived in 605 BC. These Israelites left Babylon fourteen years after the second group of returnees.

Nehemiah heard from family members who had visited Jerusalem that the people there were in trouble because the wall around the city had been broken down (Nehemiah 1:2–3). He temporarily left his position as cupbearer to King Artaxerxes and traveled to Jerusalem with the goal of rebuilding the wall (Nehemiah 2). Nehemiah, the people who returned with him, and the residents of Jerusalem managed to complete this incredible task in just fifty-two days (Nehemiah 6:15).

Just as Jerusalem needed a physical wall of protection around it, the people of God need a spiritual wall of protection around them. They needed the unseen arms of God surrounding them, not only to finish building the physical wall, but also to make a fresh start in this rebuilt Jerusalem. They needed God's help to be able to live according to His ways.

Seventy Years of Captivity

The First Temple, known as Solomon's Temple, was destroyed in 586 BC, as I previously mentioned. The Second Temple, often referred to as Zerubbabel's Temple, was rebuilt with the aid of King Darius and was completed in 515 BC. Therefore, the Second Temple came about seventy years after the destruction of the First Temple.

Jeremiah prophesied that the people of the southern kingdom of Judah would spend seventy years in captivity:

> *Therefore the LORD Almighty says this: "Because you have not listened to my words, I will summon all the peoples of the north and my servant Nebuchadnezzar king of Babylon," declares the LORD, "and I will bring them against this land and its inhabitants and against all the surrounding nations. I will completely destroy them and make them an object of horror and scorn, and an everlasting ruin. ... This whole country will become a desolate wasteland, and these nations will serve the king of Babylon seventy years."*
> *—Jeremiah 25:8–9, 11*

In a unique way, rather than counting the seventy years of captivity from the first deportation to Babylon to the first returnees to Jerusalem, I prefer to count the time from the destruction of the First Temple to the completion of the second—from 586 BC to 515 BC. The absence of the temple equates to the vacancy of God from Israel.

When God said through Jeremiah that the people would be in captivity for seventy years, I believe that He wasn't referring to the physical aspect of their captivity. Instead, He was referring to the spiritual aspect of their captivity due to the absence of the temple. God's throne among His people would be missing for seventy years.

God allowed the First Temple to be built and destroyed, but He also knew that the Second Temple would be rebuilt. This is especially interesting given the sixteen-year delay in the work on the Second Temple. As mentioned earlier, construction on the Second Temple began in 536 BC, but it soon ground to a halt and didn't resume until 520 BC.

God used the local opposition to the rebuilding of the temple—all of the people who were trying to obstruct the work and keep it from happening—to fulfill His own good purposes. The construction of the Second Temple happened in His perfect timing, just as He planned. Despite how things may have seemed at the time, God's plans were not to be thwarted.

Instead of looking at man, or even at the earthly temples that are built, we need to focus our attention on God's spiritual throne. We see this necessity illustrated further when we get to the New Testament:

Some of his disciples were remarking about how the temple was adorned with beautiful stones and with gifts dedicated to God. But Jesus said, "As for what you see here, the time will come when not one stone will be left on another; every one of them will be thrown down."

—Luke 21:5–6

The destruction of an earthen temple does not thwart the plan of God. He is not concerned about mere stones; rather, His concern is with the Messiah sitting on His throne in the Kingdom of God. That's where the heavenly Father's focus is, and that's where our focus should be.

When we embrace the perspective that God is more concerned about our spiritual lives than our physical lives, we become less focused on our physical circumstances. Whether we are free or in bondage, it really does not matter. Our aim is to watch daily for God to move in the spiritual realm.

While it may be a struggle for some to believe, our spiritual side is more important than the physical side. Jesus told His disciples in John 4:24, "God is spirit, and his worshipers must worship in the Spirit and in truth." The only way truly to commune with God is through the Spirit and not through the flesh.

The Third Temple

The first two temples have come and gone, each lasting about 500 years. When Jesus returns, a third temple will have been built in Jerusalem, and this one will last for 1,000 years. From the book of Revelation, we know that there will be a thousand-year reign of Christ on earth. (See Revelation 20:1–6; Matthew 25:31–46.)

Jesus Christ is the only One who can sit on the throne in the Third Temple, as this is the last great temple in

Israel:

> When the Son of Man comes in his glory, and all the angels
> with him, he will sit on his glorious throne. All the nations
> will be gathered before him, and he will separate the people
> one from another as a shepherd separates the sheep from
> the goats.
>
> —*Matthew 25:31–32*

> I saw thrones on which were seated those who had been
> given authority to judge. And I saw the souls of those who
> had been beheaded because of their testimony about Jesus
> and because of the word of God. They had not worshiped
> the beast or its image and had not received its mark on their
> foreheads or their hands. They came to life and reigned with
> Christ a thousand years. (The rest of the dead did not come
> to life until the thousand years were ended.) This is the first
> resurrection. Blessed and holy are those who share in the
> first resurrection. The second death has no power over
> them, but they will be priests of God and of Christ and will
> reign with him for a thousand years.
>
> —*Revelation 20:4–6*

> As I looked, thrones were set in place, and the Ancient of
> Days took his seat. His clothing was as white as snow; the
> hair of his head was white like wool. His throne was flaming
> with fire, and its wheels were all ablaze.
>
> —*Daniel 7:9*

The Importance of the Returnees' Genealogies

Chapter 2 of the book of Ezra lists the names of the
exiles who returned to Jerusalem with Ezra and helped to

repopulate the land. As we've discussed in previous chapters, the genealogies in Scripture are vital because they help to establish a sense of identity, as well as a sense of time.

In this particular context, the exiles could not claim that they had a right to Israel unless they could prove that they had descended from Abraham. Since Abraham, Isaac, and Jacob were the ones who received the promise of God, their descendants would likewise be recipients of the promise. If they couldn't prove their connection to Abraham, they were not considered true Jews and were excluded from participation in Jewish community life.

Jesus Christ would have no natural right to be called a Son of Abraham and a Son of David if there weren't proof that He came through those generations. As I'm demonstrating in this book, not only can we trace Jesus' line back to Abraham, we can go all the way back to Adam and date that line to establish that Jesus came down through 4,000 years—from Adam, through Abraham, through David, and through the Babylonian captivity—and that He truly was the Messiah that God had been promising throughout the entire Old Testament.

Because there is a historical line established, there is no argument that Jesus Christ is truly a Jew—the Son of David, the Son of Abraham, the Son of Adam. But He who is the Son of Adam is greater than Adam himself. The first Adam was full of sin, but the second Adam was full of righteousness:

So it is written: "The first man Adam became a living being"; the last Adam, a life-giving spirit. The spiritual did not come first, but the natural, and after that the spiritual. The first man was of the dust of the earth; the second man is of heaven. As was the earthly man, so are those who are of the earth; and as is the heavenly man, so also are those who are of heaven. And just as we have borne the image of the earthly man, so shall we bear the image of the heavenly man.

—1 Corinthians 15:45–49

Christ Jesus was not only a Jew; He was the exemplar of a true Jew. He was the sinless Son of God, the second Adam, the promised Messiah, who would make salvation possible for everyone who receives Him. Because Jesus gave His life as a sin offering, an exchange took place. The sins of men were given to Him in exchange for His righteousness to be given to all who would receive (2 Corinthians 5:21).

Those who walk by faith in Christ are justified by God:

For those God foreknew he also predestined to be conformed to the image of his Son, that he might be the firstborn among many brothers and sisters. And those he predestined, he also called; those he called, he also justified; those he justified, he also glorified.

—Romans 8:29–30

Everything we have in Jesus Christ enables us to enjoy the blessing of Abraham and the promises that God has been promising us ever since He first put Adam in the Garden of Eden.

Through the genealogies included in Scripture, we can see this lineage that consistently establishes the credentials of the Hebrew people and the credentials of the Messiah. They also provide important pillars and posts that help us understand that God has not been dealing with mankind for tens of thousands of years, but only for a little more than 6,000 years. If you're looking at time from God's perspective, it's only been about six days.

I believe that the seventh day, the time when Jesus Christ returns and sits on the throne in the third and final temple, is closer to us than many might think. That day will finally bring lasting peace and security to Jerusalem. The First and Second Temple each lasted about 500 years—half a day each—but the Third Temple, the millennial temple, will last a full day. God is planning to enjoy His time living among men once again. Remember Eden!

Wait for God's Timing

What an amazing God we worship. In times of trouble, may we be encouraged to turn our eyes away from our physical circumstances and look for what God is doing in the spiritual realm. Remember, His concern is with the spiritual, not the physical.

Understanding where God's priorities lie helps us to endure difficult times with patience, hope, and expectation. As we wait for Him to resolve our life circumstances in His perfect timing—and ultimately, as we wait for the seventh day—let us hold to our unwavering faith in the on-time God we serve.

Chapter Six Questions

Question: Many of God's people became comfortable in their captivity and assimilated into the heathen culture around them. Only a remnant returned to their homeland. Are you comfortable living in the world and its system? In what ways would others say that you are different from the world around you? Do you look forward to Christ's return and to heaven, or do you prefer life as you know it in the here and now?

_____

_____

_____

_____

_____

_____

_____

_____

_____

_____

_____

Question: In times of trouble, may we be encouraged to turn our eyes away from our physical circumstances and look for what God is doing in the spiritual realm. What are some difficult physical situations that you are in right now? What might God be doing in the spiritual realm in spite of—or even because of and through—those situations?

_____

_____

_____

_____

_____

_____

_____

_____

_____

_____

_____

Action: Acts 13:36 says, "Now when David had served God's purpose in his own generation, he fell asleep...." Make a list of some of God's purposes in placing you in this generation. What important work needs to be done in the time and place where God has you right now? How, like Esther, are you called "for such a time as this" (Esther 4:14)?

Chapter Six Notes

_____

_____

_____

_____

_____

_____

_____

_____

_____

_____

_____

_____

_____

_____

_____

_____

_____

_____

_____

_____

CHAPTER SEVEN

The Silent Years: Shealtiel to Jesus

During the time between the Old Testament and the New Testament—the appropriately named "silent years"—God was not actively speaking to His people. Much of what we know about this period comes from extrabiblical evidence, rather than from Scripture.

The most important thing to understand here is that throughout redemption history, God repeatedly tried to get His people to a place where they looked only to Him. After all of the exciting events that had taken place in Scripture up to this point, God took a different approach with mankind: He went silent. There was no longer any divine word from heaven to men at this time.

God Does Not Forget His People

When God allowed the people of Judah to be sent into captivity in Babylon, it might have seemed like He had forgotten about them. Do you remember when the psalmist exclaimed, "By the rivers of Babylon we sat and wept when we remembered Zion.... How can we sing the songs of the LORD while in a foreign land?" (Psalm 137:1, 4)? But no, God did not forget. He orchestrated time, circumstance, and opportunity to preserve His people and to set the rescue mission in motion.

The genealogy of Jesus Christ in Matthew 1 is a reminder that God did not forget His promise to Abraham, Isaac, and Jacob. Despite the exile, God was going to provide for people to be in the lineage of Christ—those who would make it possible for the Messiah to be born into this world at the right time according to the Father's schedule.

At times God may seem silent, but He is still present and at work in the world. Check out the story of Esther. God is still providing people to fill in that sacred lineage. As the body of Christ, the universal church, believers are also helping to continue that lineage. We are part of that continuous line to make sure that the witness to the Messiah is fulfilled as God grafts the gentiles into His people.

Right now, in this church age, we are in the times of the gentiles. Luke 21:24 tells us, "Jerusalem will be trampled on by the Gentiles until the times of the Gentiles are fulfilled." The text speaks of such a time. The time frame of this period is understood as running from Israel's rejection of Jesus Christ as Savior to the period of the tribulation.

It's during this age that the church is carrying the load of the Kingdom and witnessing to the reality of Jesus. It's the period of grafting in the gentiles whom Jesus and Paul spoke about. This is a time for the people of Israel to get themselves together, because once we reach the tribulation and the other events of the book of Revelation, God's focus will shift back to them, as He remembers His promise to them and preserves a remnant. We praise the name of God because He never forgets. He constantly remembers His Word, and He always does what He intends to do. God cannot lie; He will keep His promises.

The Last Kings of Judah

To understand the silent years properly, we need to go back and take a closer look at the last kings of Judah, who reigned before the final deportation to Babylon.

King Jehoiachin was taken captive by the Babylonian king Nebuchadnezzar, so he's often referred to as "Jehoiachin the Captive." According to 2 Kings 24:8, Jehoiachin was eighteen years old when he took the throne, and his reign lasted three months, from December 598 BC to March 597 BC.[28]

When Nebuchadnezzar made his second trip to Jerusalem in 597 BC, he took Jehoiachin back to Babylon with him:[29]

Jehoiachin king of Judah, his mother, his attendants, his nobles and his officials all surrendered to him.

In the eighth year of the reign of the king of Babylon, he took Jehoiachin prisoner. As the LORD had declared, Nebuchadnezzar removed the treasures from the temple of the LORD and from the royal palace, and cut up the gold articles that Solomon king of Israel had made for the temple of the LORD.
—2 Kings 24:12–13

Jerusalem fell into the hands of Nebuchadnezzar on March 16, 597 BC. He set up Zedekiah, Jehoiachin's uncle, as king (2 Kings 24:17). Zedekiah reigned from 597 BC to 586 BC, when Nebuchadnezzar went to Jerusalem a third time and destroyed the temple.[30]

Jehoiachin and Zedekiah were the last two kings in Judah. Following their reigns, Israel was in total captivity in Babylon.

Shealtiel

We then come to Shealtiel, the oldest son of Jehoiachin the Captive (1 Chronicles 3:17). Nebuchadnezzar did not appear to have been very interested in Shealtiel, but God certainly was. Shealtiel eventually became the father of Zerubbabel (Matthew 1:12), and it was Zerubbabel who led the first wave of returnees to Jerusalem. God works in mysterious ways!

Though Shealtiel was born just prior to captivity and never reigned, the royal line continued despite the exile. God promised David that he would always have someone in that lineage, and the anointing on Shealtiel's life shows that God was continuing to work out His promise, which would culminate with the coming Messiah. God is faithful, and He remembers His promises.

Zerubbabel and the Year of Jubilee

Working forward from 966 BC, the date we have for 1 Kings 6:1, Zerubbabel led the first wave of returnees to Jerusalem in 538 BC. In 539 BC, Darius the Mede had taken Babylon without a fight. In 538 BC, Cyrus issued a decree ordering the restoration of Jerusalem, allowing the Jews to return to Jerusalem and rebuild the temple.

Zerubbabel laid the foundation for the Second Temple in 536 BC, fifty years after the Babylonians destroyed the First Temple in 586 BC. The amount of time that passed between the destruction of the First Temple and the beginning of construction on the Second Temple is extremely important. As we have previously discussed, fifty years equates to a Jubilee celebration. The Year of Jubilee is mentioned in Leviticus 25. An actual Jubilee year appears to have occurred in 572 BC in the time of Ezekiel the priest. Let's dig a little deeper into the Jubilee celebration.

Leviticus 25:39–55 provides instructions for how Israelites who were slaves could be redeemed. The chapter concludes:

Even if someone is not redeemed in any of these ways, they and their children are to be released in the Year of Jubilee, for the Israelites belong to me as servants. They are my servants, whom I brought out of Egypt. I am the LORD your God.
—Leviticus 25:54–55

God made it clear that He would not allow any Israelite to remain a slave or captive forever. God pronounced times of forgiveness throughout Israel and made release of property mandatory. During these times, debt was forgiven, and people and lands were restored. By releasing His people from captivity in Babylon after fifty years— one Jubilee—God was abiding by His own law.

The Father would not allow His people to be away from Him longer than a Jubilee. He orchestrated their return by putting it on the heart of Cyrus, a pagan Medo-Persian king, to let the Israelites go free. God also put it on Zerubbabel's heart to lead that first wave of returnees to Jerusalem and begin work on the temple.

Four Hundred Years of Silence

Once Zerubbabel exited the scene, there is little, if any, biblical record of the remaining people in Jesus' genealogy in Matthew 1. Between the Old Testament and the New Testament, there were four centuries during which God did not speak to His people.

Sometimes God stops talking because He has said enough already. His people had not been listening, so He said nothing for a while. The silence of God may drive some crazy and break their faith, but His silence is meant to encourage people to seek Him and to look more closely at what He has already said. God's people need to obey first things first.

The Promised Deliverer

There is definitely merit in reflecting on God's Word and the order in which He has done things. When we look at the genealogy God has given us for Jesus Christ in Matthew 1, we see that Abraham, Isaac, and Jacob are mentioned, but not Joseph (Matthew 1:2).

As we've discussed previously, my theory is that even though Joseph was born an Israelite, he became an

Egyptian and lived out his days in that country. Though God did not repeat to Joseph the promise He gave to Abraham, Isaac, and Jacob, He did use Joseph to preserve the Messiah's line by providing food for the Israelites during the famine (Genesis 47, 50:20–21).

Note the symmetry of God and Scripture. When I look back at the beginning, I see Jacob and Joseph, followed by Israel's deliverer, Moses. Looking at the end of the genealogy in Matthew 1, I see God making an interesting theological point. The last three names in the genealogy are Jacob, Joseph, and the true Deliverer, Jesus (Matthew 1:16). I love how God throws in points of information so subtly.

There is order to God's ways. He has a way of reminding us of His greatness and that He will do in the future what He has done in the past. This time, He is not just bringing a deliverer; He is bringing the Messiah Himself.

Daniel's Prophecies

Before we delve into the life of Jesus, let's get a handle on some major extrabiblical events that took place during the intertestamental period. This period, which was approximately 444 BC to Christ's birth in 5 BC, is between the book of Malachi in the Old Testament and the Gospel of Matthew in the New Testament. There had been no communication from God since the prophet Malachi left the scene. So when Elizabeth and her husband, Zechariah the priest, received word from the angel Gabriel that a child was to be born, they were overjoyed for more than one reason.

We get a foretaste of what would happen during the intertestamental period from the book of Daniel:

> Then I heard a holy one speaking, and another holy one said to him, "How long will it take for the vision to be fulfilled—the vision concerning the daily sacrifice, the rebellion that causes desolation, the surrender of the sanctuary and the trampling underfoot of the LORD's people?"
>
> He said to me, "It will take 2,300 evenings and mornings; then the sanctuary will be reconsecrated."
>
> —Daniel 8:13–14

Daniel prophesied that there would be a rebellion that caused the desecration of the temple by heathen people. The days of desecration took place from 171 BC to 165 BC,[31] during the time of the Maccabees. Sixty-nine of Daniel's vision of seventy weeks had already occurred, and the majority of these weeks occurred during the intertestamental period.

The time of Israel as an autonomous nation drew rapidly to a close after the people's return under the Medo-Persians to build and repopulate Jerusalem. In 333 BC, Israel fell to the Greeks, and in 323 BC to the Egyptians.[32]

In 204 BC, Antiochus III the Great of Syria captured Israel.[33] His son and successor, Antiochus IV Epiphanes—also known as Antiochus Epimanes or Antiochus the Mad[34]—persecuted the Jews, sold the priesthood to the highest bidder, and, in 168 BC, desecrated the Holy of Holies within the temple.[35]

This last act prompted an uprising led by Judas Maccabeus. From 171 BC to 165 BC, Judas led a rebellion against Antiochus IV Epiphanes, took back Jerusalem, and cleansed the temple. He was furious that an outsider would desecrate the temple of the Lord in such a way.[36] Judas's zeal for the Lord's temple foreshadowed that which was displayed by Jesus:

> In the temple courts he found people selling cattle, sheep and doves, and others sitting at tables exchanging money. So he made a whip out of cords, and drove all from the temple courts, both sheep and cattle; he scattered the coins of the money changers and overturned their tables. To those who sold doves he said, "Get these out of here! Stop turning my Father's house into a market!"
>
> **—John 2:14–16**

God doesn't need an entire army at His disposal; all He needs is a remnant that is willing to fight for Him. Through that remnant of people who are committed to honoring His holiness and remembering His name and what He has done, He will accomplish His purposes.

Despite the efforts of Judas Maccabeus to maintain the sanctity of the temple, about a century later, the Roman general Pompey entered the Holy of Holies while besieging Jerusalem.[37] Though Pompey didn't ransack the temple or sacrifice a pig on the altar like Antiochus IV Epiphanes did, entering the Holy of Holies was still an act of desecration.

Herod the (Not So) Great

After so many rulers and officials violated the sanctity of the temple, Herod the Great must initially have been a breath of fresh air for the Jews. Born in 73 BC to Antipater the Idumean, a Jew of Idumean descent, Herod the Great reigned from 40 BC to 4 BC. As the self-proclaimed king of the Jews, he reconstructed a portion of the temple and also reconstructed the city of Jerusalem itself.[38]

Unfortunately, any sense of relief the Jews might have felt at having a Jewish ruler was short-lived. Herod the Great was so paranoid about rivals that he had a portion of his family killed so that no one would contest his throne.[39] It's no wonder that when the wise men showed up at his palace looking for the one who had "been born king of the Jews," Herod became completely unraveled (Matthew 2:1–3).

He checked with the chief priests and the teachers of the law and informed the wise men that the Messiah was to be born in Bethlehem (Matthew 2:4–8). He asked them to let him know when they found the child so that he could worship Him.

Herod, however, had no intention of worshiping the Messiah. His plan was to kill the Child King so that He could not grow up and take the kingdom—everything he had built, everything he had restored—away from him.

Herod serves as another reminder that men can become full of themselves and believe that their works make them great. God uses unsaved men and women all the time to do His bidding. But if they are not spiritually in the fold of God, He will only use them for a brief period of time. The Father will bring about His divine plan, which is more spiritual than it is physical.

The Birth of Christ

When exactly did Jesus enter the picture? We're able to determine the year with a good amount of accuracy. The census mentioned in Luke 2, which prompted Joseph and Mary to travel to Bethlehem, was issued by Caesar Augustus in 6 BC.[40] Herod the Great died in 4 BC.[41]

Since Scripture tells us that Herod wanted to kill Jesus, we know that Jesus had to be born before 4 BC. Herod's orders were "to kill all the boys in Bethlehem and its vicinity who were two years old and under, in accordance with the time he had learned from the Magi" (Matthew 2:16), so we know that Jesus fell into that age range.

We know that Jesus was born in the fall of the year because "there were shepherds living out in the fields nearby, keeping watch over their flocks at night" (Luke 2:8). The shepherds would live out in the fields until the equivalent of the month of September,[42] meaning that Jesus would have been born before the end of September.

Israel has two calendar systems. There is a civil calendar that runs from September to October (Tishri), and there is a religious calendar that runs from March to April (Nisan). According to the Jewish calendar, spring marks the start of a new religious year.[43] Jesus could have been born any time from 6 BC to 4 BC. However, with the help of the timeline, we know that Jesus lived to be thirty-three and a half years old. He died at Passover time, which is in the spring, meaning that He was born in the fall. I will suggest, with good reason, that Jesus died at Passover in AD 30. Putting it all together, the Messiah was born in 5 BC in the fall of the year.

One more point here: there is no year called "0." If going from BC to AD (BCE–ACE), time goes from 1 BC to
AD 1, according to the Jewish calendar year and not the
religious year. Here's how this goes:

- 5 BC – Birth of Christ, fall of the year
- 4 BC – Year 1
- 3 BC – Year 2
- 2 BC – Year 3
- 1 BC – Year 4
- AD 1 – Year 5
- AD 2 – Year 6
- AD 3 – Year 7
- AD 4 – Year 8
- AD 5 – Year 9
- AD 6 – Year 10
- AD 7 – Year 11
- AD 8 – Year 12
- AD 9 – Year 13
- AD 10 – Year 14
- AD 11 – Year 15
- AD 12 – Year 16
- AD 13 – Year 17
- AD 14 – Year 18
- AD 15 – Year 19
- AD 16 – Year 20
- AD 17 – Year 21
- AD 18 – Year 22
- AD 19 – Year 23
- AD 20 – Year 24
- AD 21 – Year 25

- AD 22 – Year 26
- AD 23 – Year 27
- AD 24 – Year 28
- AD 25 – Year 29
- AD 26 – Year 30 of Jesus' ministry began in the fall.
- AD 27 – Year 31
- AD 28 – Year 32
- AD 29 – Year 33
- AD 30 – Year 33½, Jesus was crucified in the spring at Passover.

By the time the wise men reached Jesus, some time had passed:

> *After they had heard the king, they went on their way, and the star they had seen when it rose went ahead of them until it stopped over the place where the child was. When they saw the star, they were overjoyed. On coming to the house, they saw the child with his mother Mary, and they bowed down and worshiped him. Then they opened their treasures and presented him with gifts of gold, frankincense and myrrh.*
>
> **—Matthew 2:9–11**

Instead of being a baby in a manger, like when the shepherds visited Him in Luke 2:15–16, Jesus was a child living in a house with His parents when the wise men finally reached Him.

It's at this point that Herod, realizing that the magi would not disclose the identity of the Messiah to him, gave orders to kill all of the boys two years old and younger in Bethlehem and the surrounding area. This prompted an angel of the Lord to warn Joseph to take his family and flee to Egypt to escape Herod's wrath (Matthew 2:13).

By combining the information in the birth narratives in Matthew 1–2 and Luke 2, we get a more complete picture of the timing of the events surrounding Jesus' birth, infancy, and early childhood.

The Gospel According to Genesis

We can see that God has woven throughout the Old Testament the scarlet thread of the Messiah and the redemption He would bring. That thread has its beginning in Genesis 3:15, a verse known as the *protoevangelium*,[44] or the first gospel.

In this verse, God addressed the serpent:

> *And I will put enmity between you and the woman, and between your offspring and hers; he will crush your head, and you will strike his heel.*
> **—Genesis 3:15**

The promised offspring who would crush the serpent's head is Jesus Christ, the Messiah, and the serpent who would strike His heel is Satan. Though God permitted Satan to harm Jesus, even to kill Him, God used Satan's actions to fulfill His plans for mankind's redemption. Though Satan struck the Messiah, God raised Him up.

God has woven this scarlet thread, the mystery of Christ, throughout the Old Testament, and when we line it up alongside historical dates and events, we see that God has proven to be faithful.

From God's perspective of time, the Old Testament encompassed four days' worth of events. We have two days' worth of events in the age of the church, the time of the gentiles, in which we now live and participate. So far, we have experienced six days of God's time, but a seventh day is coming.

The book of Revelation looks ahead to a time yet to come when God will take His day of rest as the Messiah, who descended through 4,000 years of history, all the way from the first Adam. He will claim His rightful throne and reign for 1,000 years (Revelation 20:6)—that is, one day.

Though we may be upset by the sacrilegious acts of Antiochus IV Epiphanes and Pompey, it's important to remember that the Jews themselves had also committed sacrilege in the temple. In Ezekiel 8, a messenger from God showed the prophet how God's people were desecrating His temple by worshiping other gods in it:

He then brought me into the inner court of the house of the LORD, and there at the entrance to the temple, between the portico and the altar, were about twenty-five men. With their backs toward the temple of the LORD and their faces toward the east, they were bowing down to the sun in the east.

He said to me, "Have you seen this, son of man? Is it a trivial matter for the people of Judah to do the detestable things they are doing here?"

—Ezekiel 8:16–17

Jesus drove out the money-changers and sellers of animals who were polluting the original purpose of the temple: to worship God. They had turned the practices of the temple into a money exchange. Jesus cleared the temple not once, but twice.

When Jesus returns, there will be a third temple (Revelation 11:19), which will be greater than the first two temples. Here, God will be worshiped as He is meant to be worshiped because Christ will be on the throne. There will be no sacrilege. For 1,000 years, there will be peace.

After the 1,000 years ends, the devil will be released, and there will be one last uprising against God (Revelation 20:2–3). Jesus Christ will put down that uprising, and then His people will walk into eternity with Him. God will finally have His throne among us.

The Old Testament sets us up for the climax of the New Testament: the Messiah comes not once, but twice. At His first appearance, Jesus delivered us from our sins and from living in opposition to God. At His second appearance, Jesus will sit on His throne as "King of Kings and Lord of Lords" (Revelation 19:16). As the heavenly host declared, "Glory to God in the highest, and on earth peace, goodwill toward men!" (Luke 2:13–14 NKJV).

WORKBOOK

Chapter Seven Questions

Question: To the godly Jews waiting for their Messiah, the Babylonian captivity must have seemed like the end of their hopes and prayers. How was God still at work and still extending mercy and grace to them? How do we know that God's people did not give up on seeing the fulfillment of His promises?

_____

_____

_____

_____

_____

_____

_____

_____

_____

_____

_____

Question: List some reasons for God's silence. Has there been a time in your life when God has been silent regarding your situation? How did you respond to His silence? What did you learn through it?

_____

_____

_____

_____

_____

_____

_____

_____

_____

_____

Action: Do a study on the First Temple and the Second Temple. What were the differences and similarities? What was the layout of the buildings, and what items were inside? How did each part of the temple point to the coming Messiah?

Chapter Seven Notes

_____

_____

_____

_____

_____

_____

_____

_____

_____

_____

_____

_____

_____

_____

_____

_____

_____

_____

_____

_____

_____

_____

CHAPTER EIGHT

Jesus

We came to the conclusion in the previous chapter that the birth of Jesus occurred in the fall of 5 BC. We calculated this date in accordance with the timeline provided by Scripture and extrabiblical events that took place in Israel. However, we can run into some confusion when looking at our modern calendar.

Anno Domini

The main issue we face comes from the dating of the anno Domini (AD) era, a concept introduced in AD 525 by Dionysius Exiguus, a theologian, mathematician, and astronomer.[45]

At that time, the Julian calendar was in widespread use. The Council of Nicaea had established in AD 325 that Easter should be celebrated on the first Sunday after the first full moon on or after the northern vernal equinox.[46] Due to the repetition of too many leap years, the Julian calendar was not in sync with astronomical events like the equinox, causing problems for the church by making it difficult to calculate the date for Easter each year.[47]

Pope St. John I asked Dionysius Exiguus to help resolve this issue, which he did by devising new calculations for determining the date of Easter. When he recorded the dates of upcoming Easters in his calculation table, he labeled the years in his Easter table as *anno Domini*, which means "in the year of the Lord." This new table was based on a new dating system he had devised that incorporated the incarnation of Christ—an event that he indicated had taken place 525 years previously.[48]

This dating system was further developed and applied to the Julian calendar and to the Gregorian calendar, which we use today.[49] Unfortunately, because of Dionysius Exiguus, the anno Domini system sets the year of Jesus' birth at AD 1, making it four years off from the year of 5 BC that we've determined. (Please review information in the previous chapter regarding a timeline of the life of Jesus.)

The distinctions of BC (before Christ) and AD have fallen out of use in academia, having been replaced by BCE (before the Common Era) and ACE (after the Common Era), but this dating system still acknowledges the Common Era as beginning with the birth of Christ.[50]

It's very common for dating systems to use an important historical event as their focal point. That's why the books of 1 and 2 Kings and 1 and 2 Chronicles are written the way they are, using the kings' ascensions to give a point of reference. Using physical events only works for so long because there is a limit to how long people remember the reference events.

The birth of Jesus Christ was a very significant event in world history, not just redemptive history. This single event had enough of a lasting impact to serve as the basis for a globally accepted dating system.

The Gregorian Calendar

Instituted in 1582 by Pope Gregory XIII, the Gregorian calendar replaced the less-accurate Julian calendar.[51] Because of how the Julian calendar calculated leap years, the church continued to experience a loss of Sabbath days, and the Gregorian calendar aimed to remedy this.

To bring the calendar back into sync with the equinox, the solstice, and other astronomical events, ten days had to be dropped when switching from the Julian calendar to the Gregorian calendar. That first transitional year must have been a little disorienting, to say the least. However, it seems to have worked out.

Today, the Julian calendar lags thirteen days behind the Gregorian calendar, making it clear that the Gregorian calendar was the more accurate choice. Because we're using the Gregorian calendar to date the timeline of Scripture, we can be confident of the accuracy of our dates.

The Starting Date of Jesus' Ministry

Building on the discussion from the last chapter for dating Jesus' life, we know with great certainty a date for the start of Jesus' ministry. If we know that Jesus was born after the census but before the death of Herod in 4 BC, we can calculate His birth year. From there, we can determine a date and time for the start of His ministry.

I have calculated a date for the ministry of Jesus, which began in the fall of AD 26. Just after His thirtieth birthday, the Son of Man began to be about His Father's business. Keep your eye on Luke 4:16–21, when Jesus walked into the synagogue at the beginning of the civil year (September to October) and made His famous claim:

> *The Spirit of the Lord is on me, because he has anointed me to proclaim good news to the poor. He has sent me to proclaim freedom for the prisoners and recovery of sight for the blind, to set the oppressed free, to proclaim the year of the Lord's favor.*
> **—Luke 4:18–19**

From this, I believe that we can work our way to a specific date. It is widely agreed that Jesus was thirty-three and a half years old when He died. Since there is sufficient evidence that Jesus' ministry lasted for three and a half years, which we'll get into later, His ministry would have begun when He was about thirty years old (Luke 3:23).

Daniel's Seventy Sevens

An extremely important piece of information for dating the beginning and end of Jesus' ministry can be found in a prophecy in Daniel 9. Let's start by providing some context for the prophecy.

In this chapter, Daniel prayed to the Lord and interceded for the people of Judah who had been carried into captivity in Babylon. Though Daniel was a righteous man, he identified with the people, confessing that they had sinned as a nation and offended the righteousness of God. He acknowledged that God's anger was just and that He was right in punishing His people.

At the same time, Daniel wanted to know if God was going to turn away His anger and bring His people back to Jerusalem. God responded to Daniel's heartfelt prayer by sending the angel Gabriel with a vision of how God would restore the Israelites to their rightful homeland and bring about the coming of the Messiah.

Gabriel emphasized the importance of understanding the vision and this prophecy. As we've learned from Deuteronomy 29:29, it's important for us to understand that which God has revealed to us.

The prophecy was as follows:

Seventy "sevens" are decreed for your people and your holy city to finish transgression, to put an end to sin, to atone for wickedness, to bring in everlasting righteousness, to seal up vision and prophecy and to anoint the Most Holy Place.

Know and understand this: From the time the word goes out to restore and rebuild Jerusalem until the Anointed One, the ruler, comes, there will be seven "sevens," and sixty-two "sevens." It will be rebuilt with streets and a trench, but in times of trouble. After the sixty-two "sevens," the Anointed One will be put to death and will have nothing. The people of the ruler who will come will destroy the city and the sanctuary. The end will come like a flood: War will continue until the end, and desolations have been decreed. He will confirm a covenant with many for one "seven." In the middle of the "seven" he will put an end to sacrifice and offering. And at

> *the temple he will set up an abomination that causes deso-*
> *lation, until the end that is decreed is poured out on him.*
> *—Daniel 9:24–27*

"The Anointed One" refers to Jesus Christ, the Messiah. The "sevens" are to be understood as groupings of seven years—that is, one "seven" is equal to seven years.[52]

The seventy sevens in Daniel 9:24, a total of 490 years, are made up of the seven sevens and sixty-two sevens in verse 25 and the one seven in verse 27. However, as we can tell from the three groupings of sevens in this passage, the 490 years are not continuous. There will be a period of forty-nine years, a period of 434 years, and a period of seven years. That final period of seven years is further divided into two halves.

The final seven is generally understood to be the tribulation period in the book of Revelation.[53] Since the tribulation is associated with Christ's second coming, rather than His first coming, we only need to focus on sixty-nine sevens instead of the entire seventy. This means that we're immediately concerned with a period of 483 years.

Working backward from AD 26 as the start of Jesus' ministry and taking out 434 years, or sixty-two sevens, the math takes us to 409 BC. This date means that the book of Malachi, the final book in the Old Testament, needs to conclude by 409 BC, because the period of sixty-two sevens is dated from Malachi to the beginning of Jesus' ministry.

We still need to account for seven sevens, or forty-nine years. There is a gap of time between the seven sevens and the sixty-two sevens. Otherwise, this prophecy doesn't fit the storyline in the Old Testament. This is why it's important to understand that these three sets of sevens are not continuous.

The decree to rebuild and restore Jerusalem, mentioned in Daniel 9:25, was issued by King Cyrus in about 539 BC. With this date, that set of seven sevens works out well: 539 minus 49 brings us to 490 BC, the year in which the events recorded in the book of Nehemiah concerning the rebuilding and restoration of Jerusalem concluded.

The point of going through all of this math is to show with accuracy how the Scriptures share the mind of God with us. From the rebuilding of Jerusalem and the temple in Nehemiah's day to the beginning of the ministry of Jesus Christ, the Son of God, sixty-nine sevens occurred. The book of Daniel is correct, and there is one seven remaining.

When dating Jesus' ministry, it's crucial to recognize that the sixty-two sevens and the seven sevens are two separate, non-continuous periods of time. The sixty-nine sevens began with the decree of Cyrus in 539 BC and ended with the beginning of Jesus' ministry in AD 26. It says in Daniel 9:26 that "the Anointed One will be put to death and will have nothing." How very true that was!

How Many Passovers?

Knowing the number of Passovers that occurred during Jesus' ministry helps us to determine how long His ministry lasted. According to Scripture, there were four Passover celebrations during the ministry of Jesus. These

Passovers are recorded in the Gospel of John:

- The first Passover occurred in John 2:13–25 (April of AD 27).

- The second Passover occurred in John 5:1–3, 5–9 (April of AD 28). This one is less obvious, as the passage simply says that Jesus was in Jerusalem "for one of the Jewish festivals" (John 5:1).

- The third Passover occurred in John 6:4–14 (April of AD 29).

- The fourth and final Passover occurred in John 18:28–32 (April of AD 30). At this Passover, Jesus was "the Lamb who was slain" (Revelation 5:12 NKJV).

Jesus celebrated those first three Passovers with His disciples. On the fourth and final Passover, He became the Passover Lamb who shed His blood and redeemed mankind from their sin. Revelation 5 highlights this connection between Jesus and the sacrificial lamb:

> Then I saw a Lamb, looking as if it had been slain, standing at the center of the throne, encircled by the four living creatures and the elders. ... In a loud voice they were saying: "Worthy is the Lamb, who was slain, to receive power and wealth and wisdom and strength and honor and glory and praise!"
> **—Revelation 5: 6, 12**

Knowing that there were four Passovers during the course of Jesus' ministry tightens up the timeline even more. He began His ministry in the fall of AD 26, so by the time the first Passover occurred in April of AD 27, Jesus had been in ministry for about six months. If we recall that Jesus began His ministry in the fall of the year, we can count it off like this:

- Fall AD 26 to fall AD 27: Jesus' first year of ministry; first Passover, spring AD 27

- Fall AD 27 to fall AD 28: Jesus' second year of ministry; second Passover, spring AD 28

- Fall AD 28 to fall AD 29: Jesus' third year of ministry; third Passover, spring AD 29

- Fall AD 29 to spring AD 30: Jesus' final six months of ministry; fourth Passover, spring AD 30—Jesus is the Lamb

That's how we arrive at three and a half years for the duration of Jesus' ministry.

Why am I so convinced that Jesus' ministry began in the fall of AD 26? First of all, AD 26–27 was a Year of Jubilee.[54] It would be very fitting for Jesus to have begun His ministry in the Year of Jubilee. The text He read from the book of Isaiah in Luke 4:16–21 is a Year of Jubilee text, referencing "the year of the Lord's favor." The Year of Jubilee was built upon the Lord's favor. Jesus sounded the message to those who were listening and willing to understand that the Messiah had come.

Sabbath Years and the Year of Jubilee

Let's dig a little deeper into the concepts of the Year of Jubilee and sabbath years. The year of AD 25–26 was a sabbath year, as described in Scripture:

> The LORD said to Moses at Mount Sinai, "Speak to the Isra-elites and say to them: 'When you enter the land I am going to give you, the land itself must observe a sabbath to the LORD. For six years sow your fields, and for six years prune your vineyards and gather their crops. But in the seventh year the land is to have a year of sabbath rest, a sabbath to the LORD. Do not sow your fields or prune your vineyards. Do not reap what grows of itself or harvest the grapes of your untended vines. The land is to have a year of rest. Whatever the land yields during the sabbath year will be food for you—for yourself, your male and female servants, and the hired worker and temporary resident who live among you, as well as for your livestock and the wild animals in your land. Whatever the land produces may be eaten.'"
>
> **—Leviticus 25:1–7**

This seventh sabbath year was to be like the sabbath day when the Israelites were in the wilderness and God provided them with manna to eat:

> On the sixth day, they gathered twice as much—two omers for each person—and the leaders of the community came and reported this to Moses. He said to them, "This is what the LORD commanded: 'Tomorrow is to be a day of sabbath rest, a holy sabbath to the LORD. So bake what you want to bake and boil what you want to boil. Save whatever is left and keep it until morning.'"
>
> **—Exodus 16:22–23**

On the sixth day, God gave the Israelites twice as much so that they could rest on the seventh day and not worry about gathering manna. He implemented this same principle in the concept of the sabbath year. In the sixth year, He provided triple the harvest so that in the seventh year, they wouldn't have to worry about planting and harvesting (Leviticus 25:21). Both the people and the land could rest.

The sabbath year was very important to God because He worked for six days and rested on the seventh day. He wanted that same sort of timeline in the lives of mankind, the animals, and the land.

In the Bible, the number seven is associated with the completeness and perfection of God.[55] The seventh year was to be a sabbath year, and the fiftieth year—the year after the forty-ninth year, or seven sevens—was to be a Year of Jubilee, a year to remember God's faithfulness and promises and to give Him glory (Leviticus 25:8–12). The Year of Jubilee began at the end of the forty-ninth year and continued into the fiftieth year, giving the land a rest for not one year, but two years.

On the Day of Atonement in the Jubilee (fiftieth) year, immediately after the sabbath year ended, the people were to sound the trumpet throughout the land (Leviticus 25:9). The Day of Atonement occurred in the seventh month of the religious year—that is, September to October (Tishri). We have talked a lot about Tishri, as it is the first month of the civil year. It is awesome to put more of the story together. Jesus began His ministry on the Day of Atonement, and His life ended on the (fourth) Passover. Talk about a religious figure! There is no one better than our

Christ.

A Jubilee year was set apart as a holy time to proclaim release for those who were slaves and to return land that had been sold to its original owners. The people were able to return to the land that belonged to their ancestors and rejoin their tribes. It was cause for the people to praise the Lord and give Him glory because they knew that what God had given to their ancestors would not be in foreign hands forever.

When Jesus read that passage from Isaiah in the synagogue, He reminded everyone that the sabbath years and the Year of Jubilee were part of God's law, and God would abide by His own law.

A Pivotal Point

The beginning of Christ's ministry coincided with the transition from the sabbath year to the Year of Jubilee—a time frame He would have been fully aware of. We can narrow it down to a specific day: the tenth day of the seventh month, the month of Tishri, which happened to be Wednesday, September 11, AD 26.[56]

We know from the Julian calendar that Wednesday, September 11, AD 26, was the Day of Atonement in that Year of Jubilee.[57] At the wedding at Cana in John 2, Jesus said that it was not yet His time when His mother asked Him to help the hosts who had run out of wine. The Day of Atonement, however, would have been absolutely ideal for Him to begin His ministry.

Jesus' ministry started right after His thirtieth birthday. He would have understood that His ministry needed to take place and that He needed to be in His Father's house (Luke 2:49). On the Day of Atonement, when He read from the scroll of the prophet Isaiah in the synagogue, Jesus declared that the appointed time for the Messiah, as prophesied in Daniel 9:25, had come.

It had to happen then, in AD 26, because there was only one Year of Jubilee in Jesus' lifetime. The previous Year of Jubilee happened before He was born, and the next one wouldn't happen until after His death.

Since we can date the start of Jesus' ministry with help from Daniel's prophecies and we can figure out the duration of His ministry based on how many Passovers He celebrated, we can also date His crucifixion and His resurrection. Jesus died on April 7, AD 30, and He rose on April 9, AD 30. The sixty-nine sevens had truly ended.

Christ Brings It All Together

All of the work that we have done in dating the timeline of Scripture culminates in being able to date the life and ministry of Jesus Christ. God assigned to Him the awesome task of bringing everything together:

> ...he made known to us the mystery of his will according to his good pleasure, which he purposed in Christ, to be put into effect when the times reach their fulfillment—to bring unity to all things in heaven and on earth under Christ.
> —**Ephesians 1:9–10**

First Corinthians offers more detail:

> *Then the end will come, when he hands over the kingdom to God the Father after he has destroyed all dominion, authority and power. For he must reign until he has put all his enemies under his feet. The last enemy to be destroyed is death. For he "has put everything under his feet." Now when it says that "everything" has been put under him, it is clear that this does not include God himself, who put everything under Christ. When he has done this, then the Son himself will be made subject to him who put everything under him, so that God may be all in all.*
>
> **—1 Corinthians 15:24–28**

The first part of Jesus' assignment to bring all things together required providing a way of escape for mankind from sin. Jesus reunited man with God through the forgiveness of sin and made us acceptable to God by imparting His righteousness. This was all done through Jesus' sacrificial death on the cross. He became our Redeemer, our Christ, our Messiah, so that we could be back in communion with the Father. We were distanced from God and put out of the Garden of Eden for our sin, but now we've been brought near again through the blood of Jesus Christ (Ephesians 2:13).

The second part of Jesus' assignment to bring all things together will be accomplished at His second coming. When the end finally comes and He has brought everything together, He will kneel in submission to the Father with us and give it all to Him.

Thus far, the Scripture we've been discussing has been building up to the birth, ministry, death, and resurrection of the Messiah. We'll now start discussing Scripture that builds up to the Messiah's return.

WORKBOOK

Chapter Eight Questions

Question: A Year of Jubilee is a year to remember God's faithfulness and promises and give Him glory. What specific times in your life or church are set aside to remember God's faithfulness, meditate on His promises, and give Him glory? How can you better incorporate these three purposes into your worship patterns and holiday celebrations?

_____

_____

_____

_____

_____

_____

_____

_____

_____

_____

Question: Christ brings it all together! From the dates and times of prophecy to the significance of the Jewish holy days, sabbath years, and Year of Jubilee, Jesus gives focus, order, and meaning to human history. What are some ways that you have seen Christ bring it all together in your own life, your family, your church, or your community?

_____

_____

_____

_____

_____

_____

_____

_____

_____

_____

_____

Action: Study the biblical history and significance of the Day of Atonement and Passover. Why would Jesus choose these particular holy days to begin and complete His ministry?

Chapter Eight Notes

_____

_____

_____

_____

_____

_____

_____

_____

_____

_____

_____

_____

_____

_____

_____

_____

_____

_____

_____

_____

CHAPTER NINE

Looking Forward: Matthew 24

To have a more accurate picture and better understanding of the events prophesied in the book of Revelation, we need to look first at what Jesus told His disciples about the end times.

Scripture makes it clear that we are to be alert and aware that redemptive history is moving toward a climax. This requires patience, faith, and endurance:

So do not throw away your confidence; it will be richly rewarded. You need to persevere so that when you have done the will of God, you will receive what he has promised. For, "In just a little while, he who is coming will come and will not delay." And, "But my righteous one will live by faith. And I take no pleasure in the one who shrinks back." But we do not belong to those who shrink back and are destroyed, but to those who have faith and are saved.
—Hebrews 10:35–39

It's necessary for us to know what the endgame is and understand what God has revealed to us in Scripture about the end times. The Kingdom that is coming "cannot be shaken" (Hebrews 12:28) and is completely different from any kingdom this earth has seen. Knowing this, we can hold on to our faith no matter our circumstances, confident that we can endure because of the God we serve.

Dating the timeline of Scripture shows us that God has been faithful throughout history. Since He has been faithful in the past, we can rest assured that He will be faithful to what He has said about the end.

Matthew 24

Jesus' most detailed discourse on the end times is found in Matthew 24. Leading into this text, Jesus had made His triumphal entry into Jerusalem and grieved over the city. He and His disciples were at the temple, and His disciples were admiring the buildings, to which Jesus responded that "not one stone here will be left on another; every one will be thrown down" (Matthew 24:1–2).

From our timeline, we know that Jesus' discourse took place in AD 30, and from history we know that the temple He spoke of would be destroyed forty years later, in AD 70.[58] Herod's Temple stood from 20 BC to AD 70 and was destroyed when the Romans demolished Jerusalem. Jesus prepared His disciples for the destruction of the temple, and then He prepared them for the end of the ages.

We can break down Matthew 24 as follows:

- Verses 1–2: Jesus predicted the destruction of

the temple, which took place in AD 70.

- Verses 3–8: The disciples asked Jesus what sign would signal His coming and the end of the age, and Jesus explained what they could expect to see. As creatures built around time, we want to know when the end will be and how we can be prepared, and Jesus provided some insight into these issues.

- Verses 9–14: Jesus predicted persecution on a worldwide scale.

- Verses 15–28: Jesus talked about the great tribulation, which is discussed in greater detail in the book of Revelation. Remember the missing seven from the seventy sevens in Daniel 9? That final seven, or final week, of Daniel's vision comes into play here. The last seven is split into two periods of three and a half years each. The first period is called the tribulation. The second period, which will be more difficult than the first, is called the great tribulation.[59]

- Verses 29–31: Jesus discussed the coming of the Son of Man, often referred to as His second coming, or the *parousia*.[60] The church age will come to an end with this event. The church age began with Christ and will last until He returns. Believers are waiting for this!

- Verses 32–35: Jesus used the fig tree as an example of keeping an eye on the times.

- Verses 36–44: The exact timing of Jesus' return

is unknown. God has not revealed that information to anyone, not even His Son; He has kept that time hidden for Himself. Though we cannot pinpoint an exact date, we can estimate a time frame or, as I like to think about it, a season for His return. We need to be ready for the season of Jesus' return.

- Verses 45–51: Jesus stressed the importance of watchfulness and faithful service to the Messiah. There is a lot of work to do for the coming Kingdom, so we must watch and work while it is day (John 9:4).

Having the information in this chapter, especially that regarding the great tribulation, helps us to interpret the book of Revelation more accurately. Though Jesus didn't give His disciples everything that John saw in his vision, He set the stage for the revelation that John witnessed and recorded in the book of Revelation.

Time Is Shorter Than You Think

From 1 Kings 6:1, our key verse for dating the timeline of Scripture, we've been able to work all the way back to Adam in 4344 BC. By doing the math, we know that redemptive history has lasted about 6,000 years thus far. Since 1,000 years is like a day to the Lord (2 Peter 3:8), we can see that God has been working out the redemption of mankind for six days now. Soon it will be the seventh day, the day of rest. The end of what we know on earth is coming. God is going to do a new thing!

We must be ready for the end. Those who have ears to hear (Revelation 2:29), eyes to see, and hearts that are open to Him will be saved; they will be with God forever. For those who refuse God's generous offer of salvation, judgment is definitely coming.

The book of Revelation is really about worship and the coming judgment of God. Either we worship God now and receive the opportunity to worship Him in heaven, or we deny Him our worship now and face His judgment. Those He casts from His presence will never see or hear from Him again. There will be "weeping and gnashing of teeth" for all eternity (Matthew 24:51).

Be Aware of the Season

There are two important prophecies Jesus made in Matthew 24. The first concerned the destruction of the temple. This was the second temple, which we call Zerubbabel's Temple. Occasionally, this temple is referred to as Herod the Great's Temple because Herod renovated and expanded Zerubbabel's Temple around 20 BC. Under the leadership of Titus, who would be crowned emperor in AD 79, the Romans retook Jerusalem during the First Jewish Revolt in AD 70, destroying much of the city as well as the temple.[61]

The second prophecy concerned the return of Christ. After nearly two millennia, Jesus' return has yet to occur. The disciples, however, were not necessarily aware that there would be a large gap between the fulfillment of these two prophecies. As persecution heated up under Emperor

Nero in AD 66,[62] the Jews likely thought that they were living in the last days and Jesus would return at any moment.

We, however, can see this great gap of time between the prophecy and its fulfillment. Understanding the timeline of Scripture helps us not to lose hope and also gives us the opportunity to estimate when Jesus might return.

By looking at the timeline we have been creating, we can see that God does something awesome out of heaven every 2,000 years. It's not exactly 2,000 years, but it is close enough. For example, we have Adam in 4344 BC, Abraham in 2166 BC, and Jesus in 5 BC. Rather than looking for something to happen 2,000 years after Jesus' birth, I suggest that we should be looking for something to happen 2,000 years after His death in AD 30.

Looking at the world and the overwhelming amount of instability and evil that exists, I suggest that we all prepare our hearts for something awesome to happen as we approach AD 2030. Something could happen before or after that date. I am not prophesying as much as I am sounding the alarm. We do not know what God is doing in heaven.

Let me be perfectly clear: I am not trying to predict an exact date and time. What I'm saying is that it's important to look at the timeline of Scripture and to understand the times we are living in. Jesus will not tarry forever, so we need to get ourselves together. We must focus on faithfully serving the Messiah as we continue to live in the gap between the prophecy and its fulfillment, the space between the sixty-ninth week and the seventieth week. We need to be aware of the season we are in.

Working While We Wait

As we wait for Jesus' return, it's important to understand that waiting does not mean being idle and doing nothing. While we wait on Him, we are to watch and work. Jesus told His disciples to keep an eye out for the signs of the end times as they continued to work on behalf of the Kingdom of God. He said, "This gospel of the kingdom will be preached in the whole world as a testimony to all nations, and then the end will come" (Matthew 24:14).

We are to share the gospel with others and make disciples every time we can because Jesus' return is imminent. People need to be ready. The gospel must be preached throughout the whole world before the end comes.

People must be told that mankind has a sin problem and that the penalty for sin is death (Romans 5:8; 6:23). They must hear, "For God so loved the world that he gave his one and only Son, that whoever believes in him shall not perish but have eternal life" (John 3:16). The only cure for sin-sickness is Jesus Christ and His righteousness.

We live in a day and time when the complete Bible has been translated into more than 600 languages, and at least one portion of the Bible has been translated into more than 3,000 languages.[63] Missionaries are sharing the gospel all over the globe. People who have never heard the gospel are hearing it now and learning about Jesus Christ and His church. Understand that when the Word of God has been preached throughout the entire world, the end will come. It's coming soon.

Jesus said that when the end comes, life will be similar to how it was in the days of Noah:

> *For in the days before the flood, people were eating and drinking, marrying and giving in marriage, up to the day Noah entered the ark; and they knew nothing about what would happen until the flood came and took them all away. That is how it will be at the coming of the Son of Man.*
>
> *—Matthew 24:38–39*

When Jesus returns, people across the globe will be going through their daily routines, getting married, having families, working, and retiring. Life will be going on as usual. Then the Son of Man, Jesus Christ, will break into history again at the Father's command to set up His eternal kingdom. May we know and understand enough about the Word of God that we will not be caught off guard.

Why Does Jesus Warn Us?

Some may think that once they accept Jesus as their Lord and Savior and give their lives to God, life will be easy and run smoothly. But Jesus made it clear in Matthew 24 that following Him and working to advance His kingdom on earth would lead to suffering. Acts 14:22 states, "We must go through many hardships to enter the kingdom of God." There will be a lot of suffering before we enter the Kingdom of God, and Jesus doesn't want us to be surprised by any of it.

The message about suffering had barely left Jesus' lips when the point was driven home to His disciples. Two days later, Jesus was betrayed by Judas Iscariot, one of the twelve (Matthew 26:14–16), and He was ultimately crucified. Did the disciples understand that this was not the end of the story, but a very necessary part? The suffering of Jesus was the only way to redeem mankind. Like Him, all of the disciples would suffer before they died.

By telling His disciples what to expect in regard to the destruction of the temple, His second coming, and the end times, Jesus prepared them to have their faith strengthened before it was sorely shaken and tested. As the writer of Hebrews wrote:

> At that time his voice shook the earth, but now he has promised, "Once more I will shake not only the earth but also the heavens." The words "once more" indicate the removing of what can be shaken—that is, created things—so that what cannot be shaken may remain.
>
> Therefore, since we are receiving a kingdom that cannot be shaken, let us be thankful, and so worship God acceptably with reverence and awe, for our "God is a consuming fire."
> **—Hebrews 12:26–29**

God will shake the very foundations of the earth, but the kingdom of heaven will not and cannot be shaken. Because of this, we can remain strong in our faith, even when it seems like the bottom is dropping out of our world.

None of what Scripture tells us about the end times should shake us up, because we know that Jesus is with us "always, to the very end of the age" (Matthew 28:20). Furthermore, Psalm 4:3 declares, "Know that the LORD has set apart his faithful servant for himself; the LORD hears when I call to him." God is with us, and He hears us. If we love Him and we serve Him, we don't need to be afraid.

Receiving the Revelation

The apostle John wrote the book of Revelation in about AD 94–95,[64] sixty-five years after Jesus' death and resurrection in AD 30. John surely remembered Jesus' predictions in Matthew 24, and he would have witnessed the fulfillment of one prophecy when the temple was destroyed in AD 70.

When John received the revelation directly from Jesus Christ, he could attest to both its validity and the certainty of its fulfillment. Because John knew Jesus Christ very well when He walked on earth, John also knew that Jesus had not returned for the second time. If the Lord had returned, John surely would have recognized the Master.

John's long lifespan—longer than any of the other apostles—made him the ideal witness to receive the revelation of the second coming of Jesus Christ and what would unfold in the end times. What Jesus said in AD 30 was given to John again in AD 94–95 in much grander fashion. When God repeats Himself in Scripture, it is important to take what He is saying seriously. The end times are coming, and that is a fact.

WORKBOOK

Chapter Nine Questions

Question: Do you believe that the current era is the season for Christ's return? Why or why not? What signs and scriptures back up your belief?

_____

_____

_____

_____

_____

_____

_____

_____

_____

_____

_____

Question: Do you live ready for Christ's return, or are you mindlessly going about your business like the people in Noah's day? If Jesus came back today, would you be excited and jubilant at His coming or ashamed and regretful of your lifestyle? How are you working while you wait?

_____

_____

_____

_____

_____

_____

_____

_____

_____

_____

Action: Read the Great Commission in Matthew 28:18–20. Evaluate your involvement in both personal evangelism and short- and long-term missions. Are you in prayer for the lost and for those engaged in reaching the unreached? Are you prepared to share your testimony and to give a clear presentation of the gospel whenever needed? Are you giving financially, as you are able, to help bring Bibles and missionaries to the unsaved? Identify three to five ways you could be more faithful in fulfilling the Great Commission, and begin making those changes in your life this week.

Chapter Nine Notes

_____

_____

_____

_____

_____

_____

_____

_____

_____

_____

_____

_____

_____

_____

_____

_____

_____

_____

_____

_____

_____

CHAPTER TEN

Revelation

Throughout church history, God's people have wanted to know how the end times would unfold. Thankfully, God has provided a substantial amount of information in that regard in the book of Revelation, written by the apostle John while he was on the Isle of Patmos. The information in this book expands on Jesus' prophecies in Matthew 24.

As discussed previously, the Bible states, "But about that day or hour no one knows, not even the angels in heaven, nor the Son, but only the Father" (Matthew 24:36). God has not made known the specific date of the coming of Jesus Christ, but we can anticipate the season of His coming based on the signs provided within Revelation.

The book of Revelation is a full-alarm alert to the season that is coming, and the climax of that season is the second coming of Christ, also known as the *parousia*. We need to be prepared for that awesome day.

Remember that, according to the timeline we've worked out for Scripture, every 2,000 years there has been a great work of God that moved His divine calendar forward. As we head toward 2030—2,000 years after the death and resurrection of Christ in AD 30—it may well be that we will see more signs associated with the Revelation.

The Three Parts of Revelation

The structure of the book of Revelation is laid out in Jesus' command to John in the first chapter of the book: "Write, therefore, what you have seen, what is now and what will take place later" (Revelation 1:19).

Revelation can thus be divided into three parts:

- Chapter 1: What has been seen

- Chapters 2–3: What is now

- Chapters 4–22: What will take place later

Our focus is on the third part of the book because that portion explains what will take place in the future. The seventieth week, or the seventieth seven from Daniel 9, is intricate to what is recorded in Revelation. By the way, Daniel and John wrote more than 630 years apart from each other, but their works are complementary. Jesus, through the aid of the Holy Spirit, wants us to know certain things about end-time events.

The next great thing Christians are looking forward to on God's calendar is the *rapture*. While the specific word is not mentioned in the Bible, the event is described:

> *Brothers and sisters, we do not want you to be uninformed*
> *about those who sleep in death, so that you do not grieve*
> *like the rest of mankind, who have no hope. For we believe*
> *that Jesus died and rose again, and so we believe that God*
> *will bring with Jesus those who have fallen asleep in him.*
> *According to the Lord's word, we tell you that we who are*
> *still alive, who are left until the coming of the Lord, will cer-*
> *tainly not precede those who have fallen asleep. For the*
> *Lord himself will come down from heaven, with a loud com-*
> *mand, with the voice of the archangel and with the trumpet*
> *call of God, and the dead in Christ will rise first. After that,*
> *we who are still alive and are left will be caught up together*
> *with them in the clouds to meet the Lord in the air. And so*
> *we will be with the Lord forever.*
> **—1 Thessalonians 4:13–17**

There is no mention of the rapture in Revelation, and scholars differ in their opinions as to when the rapture will occur in the chronology of the end times. I would like to suggest that the rapture will occur after the events of Revelation 3 and before the events of Revelation 4. I say this because chapters 1–3 are concerned with what has been and what is now, and we clearly know that there has not been a meeting of the church in the air with Christ. Beginning in chapter 4 of Revelation, the scene shifts back and forth from heaven to earth and speaks of what will take place later.

Immediately following the rapture, after God takes the church out of the world and leaves the world to itself for a short span of time, the period of the *tribulation* will begin. A great truth about fallen man will be evident during the time of the tribulation. That is, a vast amount of men will not seek God, even when times are difficult and they're forced to endure many trials. What a shame to think that some of God's special creation, mankind, will not reach out to the Father no matter how rough things get on earth.

Mind you, some will be saved during the tribulation. Those who are saved and alive to experience the tumult of end-time events, however, can find solace in the words of Revelation. They need to know that the events it prophesies are part of the divine plan of God. Nothing is beyond the Father's control or outside of His knowledge.

The Tribulation

The events of the tribulation, the seventieth seven, can be found throughout Revelation 4–19. This time is also the part of Revelation that ties in with what Jesus said in Matthew 24:15–28.

Remember that the tribulation is divided into two parts:

- The tribulation, lasting three and a half years: Revelation 4–7, 17

- The great tribulation, lasting three and a half years: Revelation 8–16, 19

The scroll of the revelation that Jesus opens is "sealed with seven seals" (Revelation 5:1). The first six seals are considered part of the tribulation. The seventh seal encompasses a cascade of events, including the seven trumpets and the seven bowls. These events comprise the great tribulation, so called because the last three and a half years will be far worse than the previous three and a half years.

The book of Revelation contains numerous sets of seven. Here are seven of the most prominent examples:

- Seven churches (Revelation 1:20)

- Seven seals (Revelation 5:1)

- Seven trumpets (Revelation 8:2)

- Seven key individuals (Revelation 11–13)

- Seven bowls (Revelation 16:1)

- Seven dooms (Revelation 17–20)

- Seven new things (Revelation 21–22).

The number seven indicates completion and perfection; it is the number of God.[65] These seven sevens, which serve as an outline for the events in Revelation, indicate the perfection of God's judgment and the redemptive work that He is bringing to a close.

I have always appreciated that the book of Revelation comes with a blessing: "Blessed is the one who reads aloud the words of this prophecy, and blessed are those who hear it and take to heart what is written in it, because the time is near" (Revelation 1:3). There is a blessing in understanding what God has revealed about end-time events.

The First Coming Versus the Second Coming

When Jesus came to earth the first time, His mission was not comprehended at all. Even Jesus' disciples, who were the closest of anyone to Him, misunderstood why He had come. Their expectation was for political deliverance from Roman oppression, not spiritual deliverance from the oppression of sin. Only after the resurrection of Christ did the disciples and others begin to understand His work.

When Jesus returns, however, there will be no confusion. God has made it clear through Scripture that Jesus will bring together all things in heaven and on earth (Ephesians 1:10). God will once again make His home among mankind, as He did in the Garden of Eden and through the tabernacle and the temple. Though the Father had to separate Himself from our sin in Jesus Christ on the cross, it has always been His intention to dwell with His people.

The second time, with sin and death defeated, God will live with His people in the New Jerusalem:

I saw the Holy City, the new Jerusalem, coming down out of heaven from God, prepared as a bride beautifully dressed for her husband. And I heard a loud voice from the throne saying, "Look! God's dwelling place is now among the people, and he will dwell with them. They will be his people, and God himself will be with them and be their God. 'He will wipe every tear from their eyes. There will be no more death' or mourning or crying or pain, for the old order of things has passed away."

—Revelation 21:2–4

God will be able to make His home with us because Christ will have made all things new (Revelation 21:5). I mean this literally. God will be able to enjoy the same kind of relationship with believers that He initially enjoyed with Adam and Eve. What the first Adam destroyed the second Adam (Christ) will restore. We may not know when the end will take place, but we can certainly echo John's enthusiasm in Revelation 22:20: "Come, Lord Jesus"!

The Purpose of the Second Coming

When Jesus returns at His appointed time, in addition to bringing all things together, He will also judge the world and mankind (Revelation 20:11–15). He will finally separate those who worship Him from those who don't. After Christ has finished judging the world and those within it, we will move into the eternal period (Revelation 20:13–21:4).

Judgment and worship are the two main themes of the book of Revelation. We see judgment expressed in the form of seals, trumpets, and bowls. As these events unfold, we see the great cosmic clash between God and His Holy Trinity and the devil with his false, unholy trinity.

For those of us who worship God, there is no fear or worry regarding these judgments or what will happen after this world. Our sin has already been judged at the cross. We know what's going to happen: we will live with God and enjoy Him forever.

Those who refuse to worship God will have their sin judged at the "great white throne" judgment, which will occur at the end of the thousand-year reign of Christ on earth (Revelation 20:11–15). These nonbelievers, who did not repent and accept Jesus Christ as Savior, will be thrown into the lake of fire—the place prepared for the devil, his false prophet, and the antichrist.

The earth as we know it will pass away (Revelation 21:1). God will establish a new heaven and a new earth, and He will divide those who worship Him from those who do not. People who do not worship God and accept Jesus as Lord and Savior will be separated from Him for all eternity.

The Seventh Day

Revelation 20:1–6 describes Christ's thousand-year reign on earth—the seventh day of redemption history. Even though Christ will be seated on the throne and the devil will be confined to the abyss, there are those who will refuse to enjoy the peace He brings. They will reject Christ and His lordship.

When the devil is released from the abyss at the end of the millennium, he will lead these people, these nations, in an uprising against the Lord. They will be devoured by fire, ushering in the judgment of Satan and his unholy trinity and the judgment of the wicked at the great white throne (Revelation 20:7–10). From that point, we will enter the eternal period. Redemptive history will draw to a close, and God's plan for the salvation and restoration of mankind will be finished.

Understanding What Has Been

Knowing the timeline of Scripture helps us to maintain a sense of urgency as we approach the end-time events. Understanding how God has worked in the past gives us a foundation to anticipate how He will work in the future. The key verse of 1 Kings 6:1 anchors our timeline, enabling us to date all the way back to Adam and all the way ahead to Christ, with an eye to instilling a sense of watchfulness in regard to His second coming.

Here are the main touchstones in our chronology of Scripture:

- AD 30: Jesus' death and resurrection occurred.

- 5 BC: Jesus was born.

- 586 BC: Judah was taken captive by Babylon.

- 722 BC: Israel was taken captive by Assyria.

- 966 BC: Solomon began to build the temple of the Lord (1 Kings 6:1).

- 1446 BC–1406 BC: The exodus occurred.

- 1876 BC: Jacob took his family to Egypt—the beginning of the sojourn.

- 2006 BC: Jacob was born.

- 2066 BC: Isaac was born.

- 2166 BC: Abraham was born.

- 2688 BC: The flood occurred.

- 3288 BC: Noah was born.

- 4344 BC: Adam was created.

Having these dates laid out helps us to see God at work throughout history, as He continues to move toward His goal of restoring the relationship between Himself and mankind. God wants us to live eternally with Him. Just as the tree of life was in the Garden of Eden (Genesis 2:9), it will also be found in the new Jerusalem:

> *Then the angel showed me the river of the water of life, as clear as crystal, flowing from the throne of God and of the Lamb down the middle of the great street of the city. On each side of the river stood the tree of life, bearing twelve crops of fruit, yielding its fruit every month. And the leaves of the tree are for the healing of the nations.*
> *—Revelation 22:1–2*

Trusting What Is to Come

The story of creation that began in Genesis will finally be complete, as seen in the book of Revelation. Man, who was kicked out of the Garden and separated from God, will be restored to wholeness and brought back to Him. Man will live eternally—free from death, disease, and despair—because God will live among men. Immanuel, another name of Jesus, means "God with us." What a tremendous, unmerited honor!

God has not abandoned us. He has not left us as orphans. Jesus is coming back for us:

Do not let your hearts be troubled. You believe in God; believe also in me. My Father's house has many rooms; if that were not so, would I have told you that I am going there to prepare a place for you? And if I go and prepare a place for you, I will come back and take you to be with me that you also may be where I am.

—John 14:1–3

As we have seen through the chronology of Scripture, God is faithful. We can trust Him to keep His Word and to fulfill it in His perfect timing. Let us be faithful as well. May Jesus find us at work—sharing the gospel, making disciples, building His kingdom—when He returns.

184 · MELVIN J. WOODARD

Chapter Ten Questions

Question: There are many differing views about the timing of the rapture, the tribulation, and Christ's second coming. What attitude should Christians have while discussing differing viewpoints on these things? What are the indisputable promises from Scripture on which all believers can bank their future?

_____

_____

_____

_____

_____

_____

_____

_____

_____

_____

_____

_____

Question: Why do believers not have to fear God's judgment, the tribulation, or the second coming? How should the future fate of the lost motivate you in your witness today?

_____

_____

_____

_____

_____

_____

_____

_____

_____

_____

_____

Action: Create a timeline of the major touchstones in the chronology of Scripture. At the end (around the AD 2,000s, but undated), write "the second coming of Christ." Above or below your timeline, write a verse or statement about God's faithfulness.

Chapter Ten Notes

CONCLUSION

Make a Choice

Be merciful to those who doubt; save others by snatching them from the fire; to others show mercy, mixed with fear— hating even the clothing stained by corrupted flesh.
—Jude 1:22–23

Although the focus of this book has been on gaining understanding of the chronology of Scripture, it is my sincere hope that it has also encouraged you to reach out to those who are perishing and make every effort to snatch them from the fire. God is not slow in fulfilling His promise. Rather, "he is being patient for your sake. He does not want anyone to be destroyed, but wants everyone to repent" (2 Peter 3:9 NLT). If God doesn't want anyone to be lost, neither should we.

Remember, God does not perceive time the way we do: "With the Lord a day is like a thousand years, and a thousand years are like a day" (2 Peter 3:8). If we interpret this verse literally, an hour of God's time is equal to forty-two years of our time. If you happen to be forty-two years old,

God has given you an hour of His time and attention. Have you used that hour wisely?

You may not be given a second or third hour. Consider how many people you know who have lived to the age of 84, much less than the biblical limit of 120 years (Genesis 6:3).

Eternity is forever! It has no time limit. God gives time in the here and now to test us, to see whether we will use our allotted time wisely or waste it in frivolous ways. Time well spent is time used to the glory of God. Time wasted is that which is spent on selfish desires. That narrative is for another time because talking about the heart's desires is a major theme throughout the Bible.

Perhaps the most amazing aspect of God's creation is the free will He has bestowed upon mankind. We have the God-given opportunity to choose between right and wrong, light and darkness, good and evil, and to exhibit the choices of our hearts through our words and actions. As human beings, we have choices. The most important one is the choice between life and death (Deuteronomy 30:19–20). It's up to us.

God does not force us to love Him or to be with Him. He stands at the door of the heart and knocks (Revelation 3:20). It is our decision whether we will let God in and worship Him or reject Him and live for ourselves.

Those who reject God and His offer of salvation through Jesus Christ, those who waste their precious time on earth by glorifying themselves, will be separated from God and consigned to the lake of fire for all eternity.

Those who worship God, accept His offer of salvation through Jesus Christ, and wisely use their earthly time to bring glory to the name of God will enjoy His presence for all eternity. They will be commended by Him:

> *His master replied, "Well done, good and faithful servant! You have been faithful with a few things; I will put you in charge of many things. Come and share your master's happiness!"*
>
> **—Matthew 25:21**

The Bible is not a history book, per se. It is a record of redemptive history, of God working to restore the relationship between Himself and mankind that has been marred by sin. For the Bible to be a reliable resource for our salvation, however, God has shown us various points where it is proven historically to be correct. Scripture is shown to be true by the verifiable historical events that it touches.

We can be confident that the Bible is real and that it can be taken literally. It should be approached with respect and awe and with absolute trust in our faithful God. We need to take His offer of salvation and His warnings regarding the end times seriously.

What eternal path will you choose? I hope you choose life. And if you do, who else will you snatch from the fire?

APPENDIX A

The Key Verse: 1 Kings 6:1

First Kings 6:1 is the key to dating the Bible accurately. It is one of the only scriptures in the Old Testament that we can match to a specific date in history because it gives precise details about Solomon and the temple. By providing a solid date, 1 Kings 6:1 helps us to put together an accurate timeline of events before and after it.

Let's break down the dating information in the verse:

> *In the four hundred and eightieth year after the Israelites came out of Egypt, in the fourth year of Solomon's reign over Israel, in the month of Ziv, the second month, he began to build the temple of the LORD.*
>
> **—1 Kings 6:1**

During my studies for a doctorate in pulpit communication—which I did not complete due to shifting my focus to the dating of Scripture—I took a course with a professor who talked about finding pivotal points in Scripture that would help unlock the dates for other parts of the Bible. He gave the date for 1 Kings 6:1 as 966 BC. The verse tells us that this is 480 years after the Israelites came out of Egypt. Simple math says that 966 plus 480 is 1446 BC, which is the date of the exodus.

Being able to assign this date to the exodus helped me to realize that this event wasn't 10,000 or 20,000 years ago; it was only 1,400 years before Christ. It's a tighter window of time than many people think. It may feel like God is taking a long time, but when we look at history, we can see that He is really doing quite a lot in a short period of time.

The verse then tells us that it was the fourth year of Solomon's reign over Israel. Solomon reigned from 971 BC to 930 BC. The author of this verse was using the ascension-year dating method to calculate how many years Solomon had reigned thus far. In this method, the first year of a king's reign is considered year zero, similar to how children are not considered one-year-olds until they have lived twelve months outside of the womb.

It so happens that Judah used the ascension-year method of dating, while Israel used the non-ascension-year method of dating, which we would consider ordinary dating. In other words, if a king assumed the throne in 971 BC and the writer was using the non-ascension-year method of dating, the king's reign would be considered as beginning in 971 BC. However, if the writer was using the ascension-year method, the king's reign would be considered as beginning the following year, in 970 BC.

Even though his reign lasted from 971 BC to 930 BC, the Bible says that Solomon reigned for forty years, not forty-one years, because the writer used the dating method that was conventional in Judah and didn't include the ascension year. To calculate the fourth year of Solomon's reign, instead of starting at 971 BC, we start at 970 BC. Subtracting four years from 970 BC gives us 966 BC.

This text in 1 Kings 6:1 is critically important. It's hard to pin down dates for the Bible, a book that starts in eternity past. This key verse is one tool God has given us to help us better understand the chronology of Scripture and where He is operating in time.

APPENDIX B

Resources for Further Study

- Theodore H. Epp, *The Times of the Gentiles*, Back to the Bible (1977).

- Dr. Floyd Nolen Jones, *The Chronology of the Old Testament*, 15th edition, Master Books (2005).

- Edwin R. Thiele, *The Mysterious Numbers of the Hebrew Kings*, reprint, Kregel Academic & Professional (1994).

- William Struse, *Daniel's Seventy Weeks: The Keystone of Bible Prophecy*, in *Prophecies & Patterns*, vol. 2, PalmoniQuest (2015).

- For free charts and maps to download, go to Clarence Larkin Charts at www.clarencelarkincharts.com.

About the Author

Dr. Melvin Woodard III is currently pastor of the New Salem Baptist Church in Indianapolis, Indiana, which he founded in 2010. He is also a science teacher at Charles A. Tindley Accelerated (High) School in Indianapolis.

Since Dr. Woodard and his family first moved to Indiana in June 2006, he has received a Master of Arts in Advanced Leadership ('09), Doctor of Education in Organizational Leadership ('12), and Master of Business

Administration in Health Care Administration from Indiana Wesleyan University ('15) and an honorary Doctorate of Divinity from the International University of Ministry and Education ('13). At IWU, Dr. Woodard developed a psychometric instrument entitled the *Leadership Influence and Decision-Making Inventory* (LIDMI), based on Robert Sternberg's imbalance theory of foolishness.

Dr. Woodard had previously earned a Master of Arts in Religious Studies ('90), Master of Divinity ('93) equivalency, and Doctor of Ministry in Black Church Studies ('93) from Ashland Theological Seminary's McCreary Center for African American Religious Studies, as well as a PhD (ABD) from Cambridge University in Oxford, England ('01).

Prior to assuming full-time pastoral ministry ('06), Dr. Woodard was an Anesthesiologist Assistant for 24 years in Northeast Ohio, following graduation from Case Western Reserve University ('82). He has traveled broadly, spoken extensively, and written professionally on numerous subjects.

Dr. Woodard currently resides in Zionsville, Indiana, with his wife, Beverly, and the family dog, Precious. The couple has four grown children and two grandchildren. Dr. Woodard can be contacted by email at melvin.woodard.iii@gmail.com.

About Speak It To Book

Speak It to Book, the premier ghostwriting agency and publisher for faith-filled thought leaders, is revolutionizing how books are created and used.

We are a team of world-changing people who are passionate about making your great ideas famous.

Imagine:

- What if you had a way to beat writer's block, overcome your busy schedule, and get all those ideas out of your head?

- What if you could partner with a team to crush lack of motivation and productivity so you can get your story in front of the people who need it most?

- What if you took that next step into significance and influence, using your book to launch your platform?

- What if you could write your book with a team of professionals from start to finish?

Your ideas are meant for a wider audience. Visit www.speakittobook.com to schedule a call with our team of Jesus-loving publishing professionals today.

REFERENCES

Notes

[1] Gruden, Wayne. *Systematic Theology*. Zondervan Academic, 1984, p. 172.

[2] "Ancient Eclipse Forecasts, When Successful, Were a Powerful Means of Divining Omens for Anxious Kings." Technology Through Time, no. 32. https://www.sunearthday.nasa.gov/2006/locations/babylon.ph p.

[3] Thiele, Edwin R. *The Mysterious Numbers of the Hebrew Kings*. New revised edition. Zondervan, 1983, p. 77.

[4] "What Was Solomon's Temple?" Got Questions. https://www.gotquestions.org/Solomon-first-temple.html.

[5] "Omnitemoral." Encyclo. https://www.encyclo.co.uk/ meaning-of-omnitemporal.

[6] Peck, John A. "Did Christ Quote from the Septuagint?" Preacher's Institute. August 17, 2019. https://preachersinstitute.com/2019/08/17/did-christ-quote-from-the-septuagint/.

[7] Lawrence, Paul. "A Brief History of the Septuagint." Associates for Biblical Research. March 31, 2016.

https://biblearchaeology.org/research/new-testament-era/4022-a-brief-history-of-the-septuagint.

[8] "Genesis 11 (Septuagint Bible)." Bible Study Tools. https://www.biblestudytools.com/lxx/genesis/11.html.

[9] Thiele, *The Mysterious Numbers of the Hebrew Kings*, new revised edition (Zondervan, 1983).

[10] Young, Rodger. "When Did Solomon Die?" *Journal of the Evangelical Theological Society* 46, no. 4 (December 2003), p. 589–603. https://www.academia.edu/2158881/When_Did_Solomon_Die.

[11] Thiele, Edward R. *The Mysterious Numbers of the Hebrew Kings*. 2nd edition. Erdmans, 1965.

[12] "The Assyrian Conquests (853 bce–612 bce)." From "War," in *Gale Encyclopedia of World History*, in Encyclopedia.com. https://www.encyclopedia.com/history/encyclopedias-almanacs-transcripts-and-maps/assyrian-conquests-853-bce-612-bce.

[13] "Chronology of the Old Testament." From *Encyclopedia of the Bible*, in Bible Gateway. https://www.biblegateway.com/resources/encyclopedia-of-the-bible/Chronology-Old-Testament.

[14] "Northern Kingdom Falls to Assyria." Bible Study Tools. https://www.biblestudytools.com/commentaries/revelation/related-topics/northern-kingdom-falls-to-assyria.html.

[15] "Northern Kingdom Falls to Assyria," Bible Study Tools.

[16] Walvoord, John F. and Roy B. Zuck. *The Bible Knowledge Commentary: Old Testament* (Victory Books, 1985), p. 484.

[17] "The Destruction of Jerusalem." Bible History Online. https://www.bible-history.com/map_babylonian_captivity/map_of_the_deportation_of_judah_the_destruction_of_jerusalem.html.

[18] Walvoord and Zuck, *The Bible Knowledge Commentary: Old Testament*, p. 484.

[19] Walvoord and Zuck, *The Bible Knowledge Commentary: Old Testament*, p. 586.

[20] Walvoord and Zuck, *The Bible Knowledge Commentary: Old Testament*, p. 586.

[21] Thiele, *The Mysterious Numbers of the Hebrew Kings*, new revised edition (Zondervan, 1983).

[22] "The Cyrus Cylinder." Bible History Online. https://www.bible-history.com/archaeology/persia/cyrus-cylinder.html

[23] Graham, Ron. "Remnant Returns and Rebuilds—and Zerubbabel Leads Them." Simply Bible. 2001. https://www.simplybible.com/f639-toi-remnant-returns-rebuilds.htm.

[24] Schiffman, Lawrence H. "Building the Second Temple." My Jewish Learning. https://www.myjewishlearning.com/article/second-temple/.

[25] Graham, "Remnant Returns and Rebuilds."

[26] Walvoord and Zuck, *The Bible Knowledge Commentary: Old Testament*, p. 667.

[27] Walvoord and Zuck, *The Bible Knowledge Commentary: Old Testament*, p. 656, 658.

[28] Walvoord and Zuck, *The Bible Knowledge Commentary: Old Testament*, p. 584.

[29] Walvoord and Zuck, *The Bible Knowledge Commentary: Old Testament*, p. 586.

[30] Walvoord and Zuck, *The Bible Knowledge Commentary: Old Testament*, p. 584–586.

[31] "What Were the 400 Years of Silence?" Got Questions. https://www.gotquestions.org/400-years-of-silence.html.

[32] "4th Century B.C. – Ancient History Timeline," Bible History Online. https://www.bible-history.com/timeline/timeline_400_300_bc.html.

[33] "Antiochus III." From *Encyclopedia of World Biography*, in Encyclopedia.com. https://www.encyclopedia.com/history/encyclopedias-almanacs-transcripts-and-maps/antiochus-iii.

[34] Volkmann, Hans. "Antiochus IV Epiphanes – Selucid King." Encyclopaedia Britannica. https://www.britannica.com/biography/Antiochus-IV-Epiphanes.

[35] "Antiochus IV Epiphanes Bust." Bible History Online. https://www.bible-history.com/archaeology/greece/2-antiochus-iv-bust-bb.html.

[36] Barnes, Albert. "Daniel 8." In Barnes' Notes, 1834, in BibleHub. https://biblehub.com/commentaries/barnes/daniel/8.htm.

[37] Barnes, "Daniel 8."

[38] Cartwright, Mark. "Herod the Great." Ancient History Encyclopedia. September 12, 2016. https://www.ancient.eu/Herod_the_Great/.

[39] Perowne, Stewart Henry. "Herod King of Judea." Encyclopaedia Britannica. https://www.britannica.com/biography/Herod-king-of-Judaea.

[40] Gruen, Erich S. In Bowman, Alan K., Edward Champlin, and Andrew Lintott, eds., *The Cambridge Ancient History*, vol. 10 (Cambridge University Press, 1996), p. 157.

[41] Perowne, Steward Henry. "Herod King of Judea." Encyclopaedia Britannica. https://www.britannica.com/biography/Herod-king-of-Judaea.

[42] "When Was Jesus Born?" Bible Info. https://www.bibleinfo.com/en/questions/when-was-jesus-born.

[43] Loughran, David B. "The Sacred Calendar of the God of Israel." A Voice in the Wilderness. http://www.avoiceinthewilderness.org/saccal/cal10.html.

[44] "What Is the Protoevangelium." Got Questions. https://www.gotquestions.org/protoevangelium.html.

[45] "Dionysius Exiguus." Encyclopaedia Britannicia. https://www.britannica.com/biography/Dionysius-Exiguus.

[46] "Calculating the Easter Date." Time and Date. https://www.timeanddate.com/calendar/determining-easter-date.html.

[47] "The Julian Calendar." Time and Date. https://www.timeanddate.com/calendar/julian-calendar.html.

[48] Hunter, Margaret. "What Is the Meaning of AD, BC, BCE and CE?" Amazing Bible Timeline. April 26, 2013. https://amazingbibletimeline.com/blog/q4_ad_bc_ce_bce/.

[49] Hunter, "What Is the Meaning of AD, BC, BCE and CE?"

[50] Hunter, Margaret "What Is the Meaning of AD, BC, BCE and CE?"

[51] "Change from Julian to Gregorian Calendar." Time and Date. https://www.timeanddate.com/calendar/julian-gregorian-switch.html.

[52] "Old Testament Prophecy: The First Forty-Nine Years or 'Seven Sevens.'" Jewish Roots. https://jewishroots.net/library/prophecy/daniel/daniel-9-24-27/seven-sevens-or-49-years.html.

[53] "Daniel's 70th Week." Jewish Roots. https://jewishroots.net/library/prophecy/daniel/daniel-9-24-27/the-seventieth-week-of-daniel.html.

[54] Coulter, Fred R. *The Appointed Times of Jesus the Messiah.* York Publishing Company, 2012.

[55] "Seven Perfection, Completeness." Bible Study Tools. https://www.biblestudytools.com/commentaries/revelation/introduction/seven-perfection-completeness.html.

[56] "Calendar for September 26." Time and Date. https://www.timeanddate.com/calendar/monthly.html?year=26&month=9&country=34.

[57] Coulter, *The Appointed Times of Jesus the Messiah.*

[58] "The Romans Destroy the Temple at Jerusalem, A.D. 70." Eyewitness to History. http://www.eyewitnesstohistory.com/jewishtemple.htm.

[59] "What Is the Great Tribulation?" Got Questions. https://www.gotquestions.org/Great-Tribulation.html.

[60] Elwell, Walter A. "Entry for 'Parousia.'" In *Evangelical Dictionary of Theology* (1997), in Bible Study Tools. https://www.biblestudytools.com/dictionary/parousia/.

[61] "Titus (39 AD – 81 AD)." BBC. https://www.bbc.co.uk/history/historic_figures/titus.shtml.

[62] "Nero and the Jewish Revolt." Bible History Online. https://www.bible-history.com/nero/NEROThe_Jewish_Revolt.htm.

[63] "How Many Languages Has the Bible Been Translated Into?" Biblica. https://www.biblica.com/resources/bible-faqs/how-many-different-languages-has-the-bible-been-translated-into/.

[64] Larkin, Clarence. *The Greatest Book on Dispensational Truth in the World*. Revised and enlarged edition. Rev. Clarence Larkin Est., 1920.

[65] "Seven Perfection, Completeness," Bible Study Tools.

CPSIA information can be obtained
at www.ICGtesting.com
Printed in the USA
BVHW081539050321
601818BV00001B/162

9 781945 793929